USBORNE INTERNET-LINKED
SPANISH
DICTIONARY
FOR BEGINNERS

Helen Davies
Illustrated by John Shackell
Designed by Brian Robertson
Edited by Nicole Irving

Language consultants: Jane Straker, Gloria Brass and Marta Nuñez
Additional designs by Kim Blundell, Stephen Wright and Sarah Cronin
Editorial help from Anita Ganeri, Kate Needham, Mairi Mackinnon and Katie Daynes

Contents

(m)

(f)

About nouns

Spanish nouns are either masculine or feminine (this is called their gender). "The" is **el** when the word is masculine and **la** when it is feminine. In the plural **el** becomes **los** and **la** becomes **las**. Sometimes the following abbreviations are used: **(f)** feminine, **(m)** masculine, **(s)** singular, **(pl)** plural. In Spanish, nouns describing what people do or are (e.g. dancer) often have a masculine and a feminine form. Both forms are given in the alphabetical word list at the back of this book. Spanish words often have a mark over one of the vowels (e.g. **el balcón**). This is called a stress mark and shows that you should emphasize that part of the word. You can find out how each word sounds on the Usborne Quicklinks Web site.

About adjectives

Adjectives in Spanish change their ending depending on whether the noun they are describing is masculine or feminine. Most adjectives end in **o** in the masculine and the **o** changes to **a** in the feminine. However, it is useful to learn both masculine and feminine forms, so both are given in the word boxes. When you see only one form, it means the masculine and feminine are the same.

About verbs

Verbs in this book appear in the infinitive (e.g. "to hide" in English). In Spanish, infinitives end in either **ar**, **er** or **ir**. You can find out how to use verbs on page 99 and there is a list of irregular verbs on page 105.

2

Usborne Quicklinks

This book has its own Usborne Quicklinks Web site where you can listen to all the words and phrases read by a native Spanish speaker.

To visit the Quicklinks Web site for this book, go to **www.usborne-quicklinks.com** and enter the keywords "LA spanish dictionary for beginners".

Listening to the words

To hear the words and phrases in this book, you will need your Web browser (e.g. Internet Explorer or Netscape Navigator) and a program such as RealPlayer® or Windows® Media Player. These programs are free and, if you don't already have one of them, you can download them from Usborne Quicklinks. Your computer also needs a sound card but most computers already have one.

Picture puzzles and useful Web sites

In Usborne Quicklinks you will also find Spanish picture puzzles that you can print out for free, and links to lots of other useful Web sites where you can listen to Spanish radio, improve your Spanish grammar and find out more about the country and culture.

Disclaimer

The Usborne Quicklinks Web site contains links to external Web sites that do not belong to Usborne Publishing. The links are regularly reviewed and updated, but Usborne Publishing is not responsible for the content on any Web site other than its own. We recommend that children are supervised while on the Internet, that they do not use Internet Chat Rooms, and that you use Internet filtering software to block unsuitable material. Please ensure that children read and follow the safety guidelines displayed in Usborne Quicklinks. For more information, see the **Net Help** area on the Usborne Quicklinks Web site.

Meeting people

¡Hola!	Hello	**el hombre**	man
¡Adiós!	Goodbye	**la mujer**	woman
¡Hasta pronto!	See you later	**el bebé**	baby
dar la mano	to shake hands	**el niño**	boy
dar un beso	to kiss	**la niña**	girl

presentar	to introduce	**¿Qué tal?**	How are you?
la amiga	friend (f)	**Muy bien, gracias.**	Very well,
el amigo	friend (m)		thank you.
encontrarse con	to meet		

charlar	to chat
Sí	Yes
No	No
De acuerdo	I agree
decir	to say
reírse	to laugh

charlar

Sí

No

De acuerdo

decir

reírse

el nombre

el nombre de pila

Pilar RUIZ

el apellido

el nombre	name
el nombre de pila	first name
el apellido	surname
¿Cómo te llamas?	What's your name?
Me llamo...	My name is...
Se llama...	His name is...

Me llamo...

Se llama...

¿Cómo te llamas?

la edad

¿Cuántos años tienes?

chico

mayor que

menor que

mayor

Tengo diecinueve años

la misma edad

la edad	age	mayor	old
¿Cuántos años tienes?	How old are you?	mayor que	older than
Tengo diecinueve años	I'm nineteen	menor que	younger than
chico(a)	young	la misma edad	the same age

5

Families

la familia	family	la abuela	grandmother
el padre	father	la tía	aunt
la madre	mother	el tío	uncle
el hermano	brother	la prima	cousin (f)
la hermana	sister	el primo	cousin (m)
el abuelo	grandfather		

ser parientes	to be related	la nieta	granddaughter
el hijo	son	tenerle cariño a	to be fond of
la hija	daughter	el sobrino	nephew
criar	to bring up	la sobrina	niece
el nieto	grandson		

la esposa

el marido

los padres

querer a

la esposa	wife
el marido	husband
los padres	parents
querer a	to love
los hijos	children
los gemelos	twin brothers
el hijo único	only son

los hijos

los gemelos

el hijo único

la vida

la niñez

el casamiento

el nacimiento

nacer

casarse

la boda

la muerte

trabajar

la vejez

morirse

el entierro

a vida	life	la boda	wedding
el nacimiento	birth	trabajar	to work
nacer	to be born	la vejez	old age
a niñez	childhood	la muerte	death
el casamiento	marriage	morirse	to die
casarse	to get married	el entierro	funeral

7

Appearance and personality

bonita

guapo

fuerte

flaco

débil

delgada

gordo

bonito(a)	pretty
guapo	good-looking
fuerte	strong
débil	weak
flaco(a)	thin
delgado(a)	slim
gordo(a)	fat

tener el pelo rubio

ser calvo

...el pelo castaño

ser pelirroja

...el pelo lacio

tener el pelo rizado

...flequillo

...trenzas

tener el pelo rubio	to have blond hair	tener el pelo rizado	to have curly hair
el pelo castaño	brown hair	flequillo	bangs
ser pelirrojo(a)	to have red hair	trenzas	braids
el pelo lacio	straight hair	ser calvo	to be bald

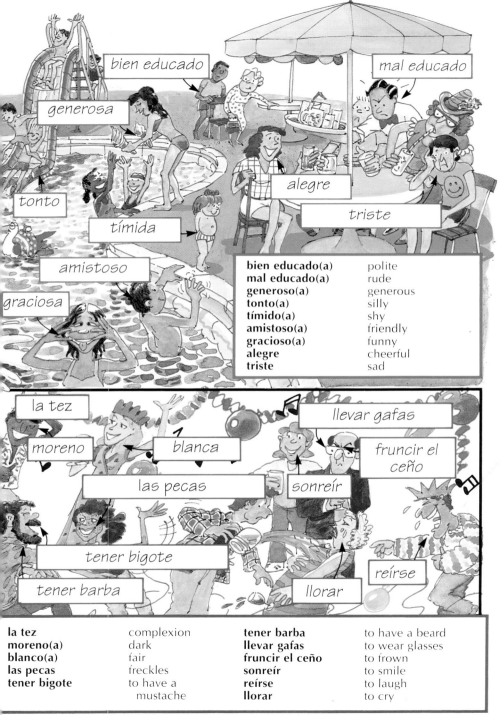

bien educado

generosa

mal educado

alegre

tonto

triste

tímida

amistoso

graciosa

bien educado(a)	polite
mal educado(a)	rude
generoso(a)	generous
tonto(a)	silly
tímido(a)	shy
amistoso(a)	friendly
gracioso(a)	funny
alegre	cheerful
triste	sad

la tez

llevar gafas

moreno

blanca

fruncir el ceño

las pecas

sonreír

tener bigote

reírse

tener barba

llorar

la tez	complexion	tener barba	to have a beard
moreno(a)	dark	llevar gafas	to wear glasses
blanco(a)	fair	fruncir el ceño	to frown
las pecas	freckles	sonreír	to smile
tener bigote	to have a mustache	reírse	to laugh
		llorar	to cry

9

Your body

la cabeza	head
el pelo	hair
la cara	face
la piel	skin
el ojo	eye
la mejilla	cheek
la nariz	nose
la oreja	ear
la boca	mouth
el diente	tooth
la lengua	tongue
el labio	lip
el cuello	neck
el mentón	chin

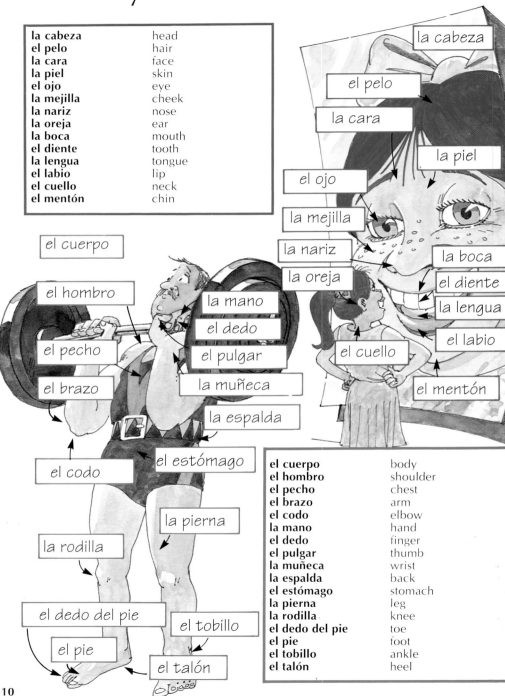

la cabeza

el pelo

la cara

el ojo

la piel

la mejilla

la nariz

la boca

la oreja

el diente

la lengua

el labio

el cuello

el mentón

el cuerpo

el hombro

la mano

el dedo

el pecho

el pulgar

el brazo

la muñeca

la espalda

el cuello

el codo

el estómago

la pierna

la rodilla

el dedo del pie

el tobillo

el pie

el talón

el cuerpo	body
el hombro	shoulder
el pecho	chest
el brazo	arm
el codo	elbow
la mano	hand
el dedo	finger
el pulgar	thumb
la muñeca	wrist
la espalda	back
el estómago	stomach
la pierna	leg
la rodilla	knee
el dedo del pie	toe
el pie	foot
el tobillo	ankle
el talón	heel

10

ser alto	to be tall
ser bajo	to be short
pesarse	to weigh yourself
ser liviano	to be light
ser pesado	to be heavy

el lado izquierdo

el lado derecho

ser alto

ser bajo

pesarse

ser liviano

ser pesado

| el lado izquierdo | left side |
| el lado derecho | right side |

arrodillarse

acostarse

estar acostado

andar descalzo

estar de rodillas

sentarse

pararse

estar parado

andar descalzo	to walk barefoot
pararse	to stand up
estar parado(a)	to be standing
arrodillarse	to kneel down
estar de rodillas	to be kneeling
acostarse	to lie down
estar acostado(a)	to be lying down
sentarse	to sit down
estar sentado(a)	to be sitting down

estar sentado

11

Houses and homes

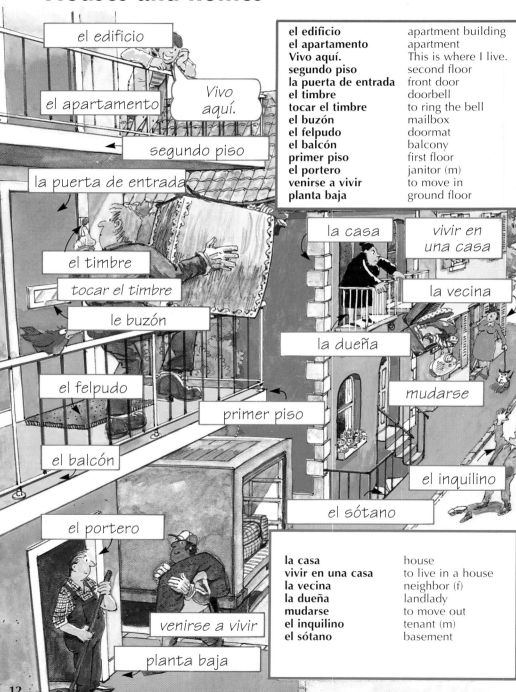

el edificio

el apartamento

Vivo aquí.

segundo piso

la puerta de entrada

el timbre

tocar el timbre

le buzón

el felpudo

el balcón

el portero

venirse a vivir

planta baja

la casa

vivir en una casa

la vecina

la dueña

mudarse

el inquilino

el sótano

primer piso

el edificio	apartment building
el apartamento	apartment
Vivo aquí.	This is where I live.
segundo piso	second floor
la puerta de entrada	front door
el timbre	doorbell
tocar el timbre	to ring the bell
el buzón	mailbox
el felpudo	doormat
el balcón	balcony
primer piso	first floor
el portero	janitor (m)
venirse a vivir	to move in
planta baja	ground floor

la casa	house
vivir en una casa	to live in a house
la vecina	neighbor (f)
la dueña	landlady
mudarse	to move out
el inquilino	tenant (m)
el sótano	basement

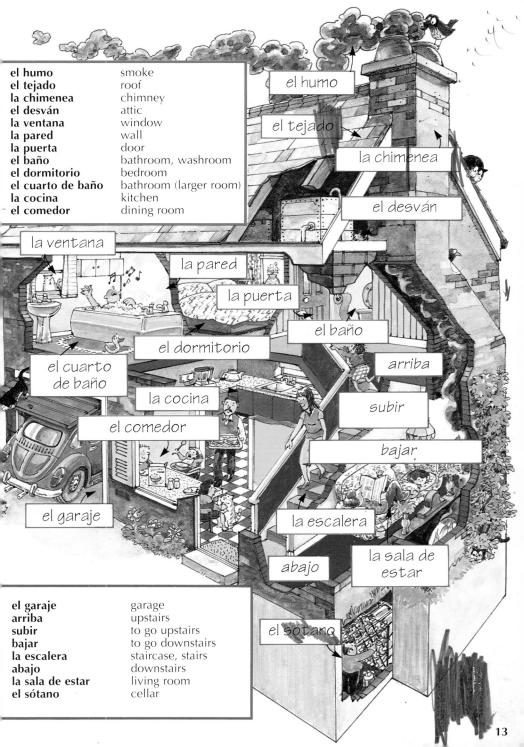

el humo	smoke
el tejado	roof
la chimenea	chimney
el desván	attic
la ventana	window
la pared	wall
la puerta	door
el baño	bathroom, washroom
el dormitorio	bedroom
el cuarto de baño	bathroom (larger room)
la cocina	kitchen
el comedor	dining room

el humo

el tejado

la chimenea

el desván

la ventana

la pared

la puerta

el baño

el dormitorio

arriba

el cuarto de baño

la cocina

subir

el comedor

bajar

el garaje

la escalera

abajo

la sala de estar

el sótano

el garaje	garage
arriba	upstairs
subir	to go upstairs
bajar	to go downstairs
la escalera	staircase, stairs
abajo	downstairs
la sala de estar	living room
el sótano	cellar

13

Dining room and living room

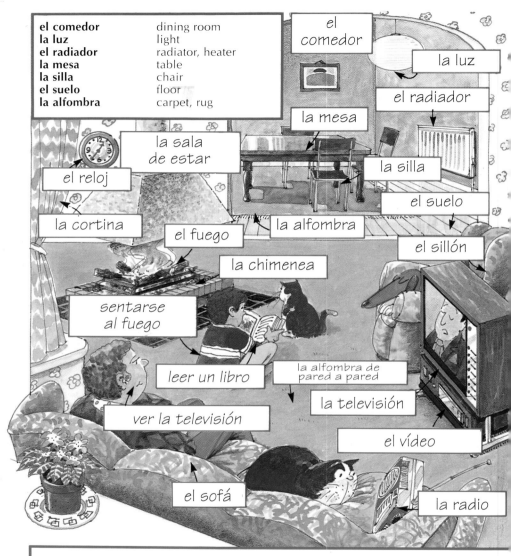

el comedor	dining room
la luz	light
el radiador	radiator, heater
la mesa	table
la silla	chair
el suelo	floor
la alfombra	carpet, rug

el comedor

la luz

el radiador

la mesa

la silla

el suelo

la sala de estar

el reloj

la cortina

el fuego

la alfombra

el sillón

la chimenea

sentarse al fuego

leer un libro

la alfombra de pared a pared

ver la televisión

la televisión

el vídeo

el sofá

la radio

la sala de estar	living room	leer un libro	to read a book
el reloj	clock	ver la televisión	to watch television
la cortina	curtain	el sofá	sofa
el fuego	fire	la alfombra de	wall-to-wall
la chimenea	fireplace	pared a pared	carpet
el sillón	armchair	la televisión	television
sentarse al fuego	to sit by the fire	el vídeo	video
		la radio	radio

In the kitchen

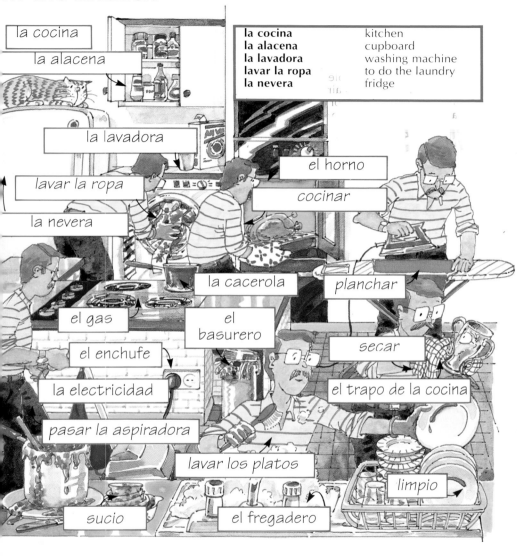

la cocina

la alacena

la lavadora

lavar la ropa

la nevera

la cocina	kitchen
la alacena	cupboard
la lavadora	washing machine
lavar la ropa	to do the laundry
la nevera	fridge

el horno

cocinar

la cacerola

planchar

el gas

el basurero

secar

el enchufe

la electricidad

el trapo de la cocina

pasar la aspiradora

lavar los platos

limpio

sucio

el fregadero

el horno	oven	pasar la aspiradora	to vacuum
cocinar	to cook	lavar los platos	to wash the
la cacerola	saucepan		dishes
el gas	gas	sucio(a)	dirty
el basurero	trash bin	el fregadero	sink
planchar	to iron	secar	to dry
el enchufe	plug	el trapo de la cocina	tea towel
la electricidad	electricity	limpio(a)	clean

15

In the backyard

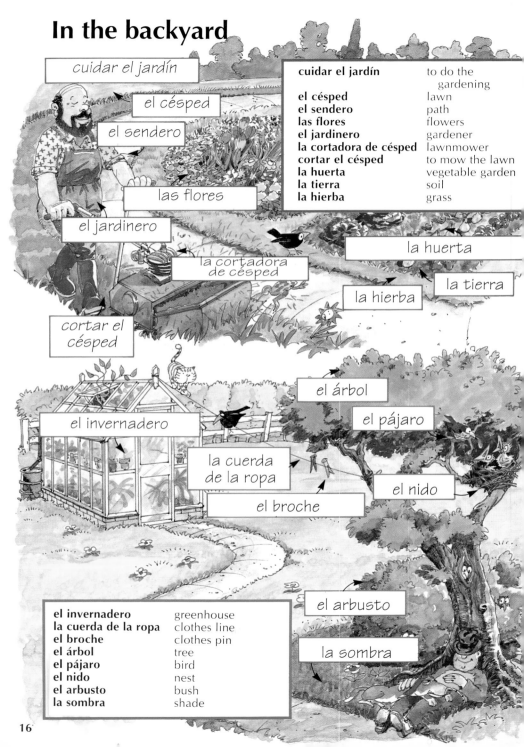

cuidar el jardín

el césped

el sendero

las flores

el jardinero

la cortadora de césped

cortar el césped

cuidar el jardín	to do the gardening
el césped	lawn
el sendero	path
las flores	flowers
el jardinero	gardener
la cortadora de césped	lawnmower
cortar el césped	to mow the lawn
la huerta	vegetable garden
la tierra	soil
la hierba	grass

la huerta

la tierra

la hierba

el árbol

el pájaro

el invernadero

la cuerda de la ropa

el nido

el broche

el arbusto

la sombra

el invernadero	greenhouse
la cuerda de la ropa	clothes line
el broche	clothes pin
el árbol	tree
el pájaro	bird
el nido	nest
el arbusto	bush
la sombra	shade

la abeja

la mariposa

la avispa

picar

oler bien

la rosa

bonita

el crisantemo

el geranio

el tulipán

el clavel

las nomeolvides

las semillas

la maleza

plantar

el bulbo

arrancar la maleza

la abeja	bee	el tulipán	tulip
la mariposa	butterfly	las nomeolvides	forget-me-nots
la avispa	wasp	el clavel	carnation
picar	to sting	las semillas	seeds
la rosa	rose	plantar	to plant
oler bien	to smell sweet	el bulbo	bulb
bonito(a)	pretty, lovely	arrancar la maleza	to weed
el crisantemo	chrysanthemum	la maleza	weeds
el geranio	geranium		

la pala

el cobertizo

la horquilla

la regadera

la carretilla

la paleta

el rastrillo

el cobertizo	garden shed
la carretilla	wheelbarrow
la paleta	trowel
el rastrillo	rake
la pala	spade
la horquilla	fork
la regadera	watering can

Pets

el perro	dog
la perrera	dog house
el cachorro	puppy
el pelo	fur
la pata	paw
juguetón	playful
ladrar	to bark
¡CUIDADO CON EL PERRO!	BEWARE OF THE DOG
perseguir	to chase
traer	to fetch
el rabo	tail
mover el rabo	to wag its tail
gruñir	to growl
llevar a pasear	to take for a walk

el perro

la perrera

el cachorro

el pelo

la pata

juguetón

ladrar

¡CUIDADO CON EL PERRO!

perseguir

traer

el rabo

mover el rabo

gruñir

llevar a pasear

el gato	cat
el cesto	basket
ronronear	to purr
el gatito	kitten
maullar	to mew
estirarse	to stretch
la garra	claw
suave	soft
encantador(a)	sweet

el gato

el cesto

ronronear

el gatito

maullar

estirarse

la garra

suave

encantador

el canario	canary	el conejo	rabbit
posarse	to perch	la tortuga	tortoise
el ala (f)*	wing	la jaula	cage
el pico	beak	dar de comer	to feed
la pluma	feather	el pez de colores	goldfish
el hámster	hamster	el ratón	mouse
el erizo	hedgehog	la pecera	fish bowl
el conejillo de Indias	guinea pig		

el canario
el ala
el hámster
posarse
el pico
la pluma
el erizo
el conejillo de Indias
el conejo
la tortuga
la jaula
el pez de colores
dar de comer
el ratón
la pecera

*You say **el ala** even though it is feminine.
This is because **el** is sometimes used instead of **la** in front of words beginning with "a" or "ha".

Getting up

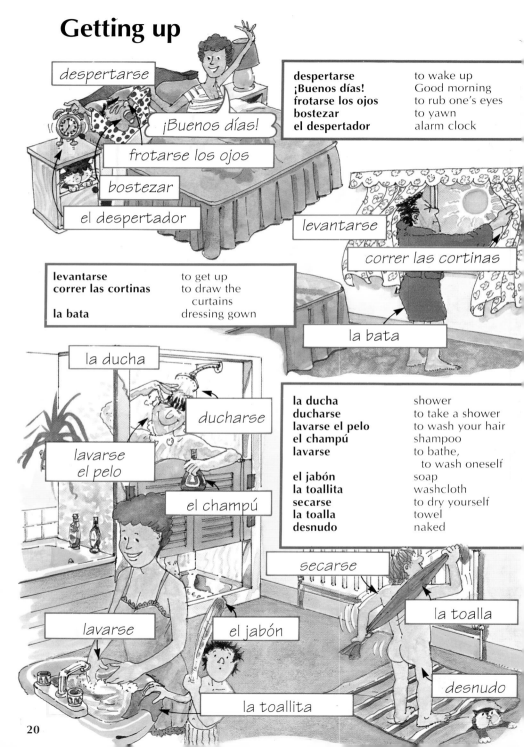

despertarse

¡Buenos días!

frotarse los ojos

bostezar

el despertador

despertarse	to wake up
¡Buenos días!	Good morning
frotarse los ojos	to rub one's eyes
bostezar	to yawn
el despertador	alarm clock

levantarse

correr las cortinas

levantarse	to get up
correr las cortinas	to draw the curtains
la bata	dressing gown

la bata

la ducha

ducharse

lavarse el pelo

el champú

la ducha	shower
ducharse	to take a shower
lavarse el pelo	to wash your hair
el champú	shampoo
lavarse	to bathe, to wash oneself
el jabón	soap
la toallita	washcloth
secarse	to dry yourself
la toalla	towel
desnudo	naked

secarse

la toalla

lavarse

el jabón

desnudo

la toallita

20

afeitarse	to shave
el espejo	mirror
la maquinilla eléctrica	electric razor
la máquina de afeitar	razor
la espuma de afeitar	shaving cream

afeitarse

el espejo

la maquinilla eléctrica

la máquina de afeitar

la espuma de afeitar

el agua caliente

el agua fría

el grifo

la pasta de dientes

el cepillo de dientes

lavarse los dientes

el grifo	faucet
el agua (f) caliente	hot water
el agua fría	cold water
la pasta de dientes	toothpaste
el cepillo de dientes	toothbrush
lavarse los dientes	to brush your teeth

secarse el pelo	to dry your hair
el secador	hairdryer
el cepillo	brush
el peine	comb
peinarse	to comb your hair
cepillarse el pelo	to brush your hair

secarse el pelo

el secador

el cepillo

el peine

maquillarse

el rímel

peinarse

cepillarse el pelo

la base

el lápiz de labios

el perfume

maquillarse	to put on make-up
el rímel	mascara
la base	foundation
el lápiz de labios	lipstick
el perfume	perfume

Clothes

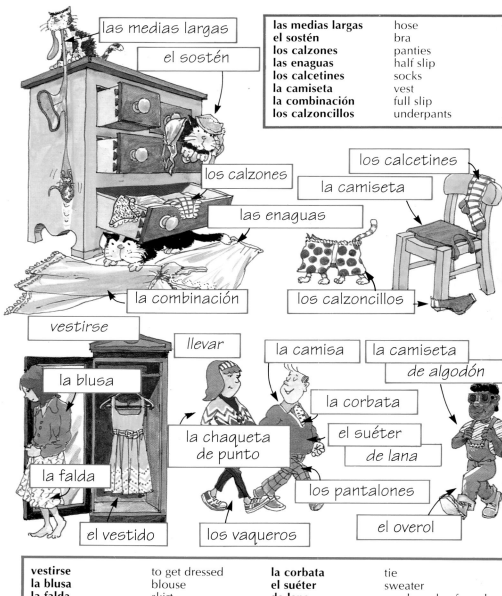

las medias largas

el sostén

las medias largas	hose
el sostén	bra
los calzones	panties
las enaguas	half slip
los calcetines	socks
la camiseta	vest
la combinación	full slip
los calzoncillos	underpants

los calzones

los calcetines

la camiseta

las enaguas

la combinación

los calzoncillos

vestirse

llevar

la camisa

la camiseta de algodón

la blusa

la corbata

la chaqueta de punto

el suéter de lana

la falda

los pantalones

el vestido

los vaqueros

el overol

vestirse	to get dressed	**la corbata**	tie
la blusa	blouse	**el suéter**	sweater
la falda	skirt	**de lana**	wool, made of wool
el vestido	dress	**los pantalones**	pants
llevar	to wear	**la camiseta**	T-shirt
la chaqueta de punto	cardigan	**de algodón**	cotton,
los vaqueros	jeans		made of cotton
la camisa	shirt	**el overol**	overalls

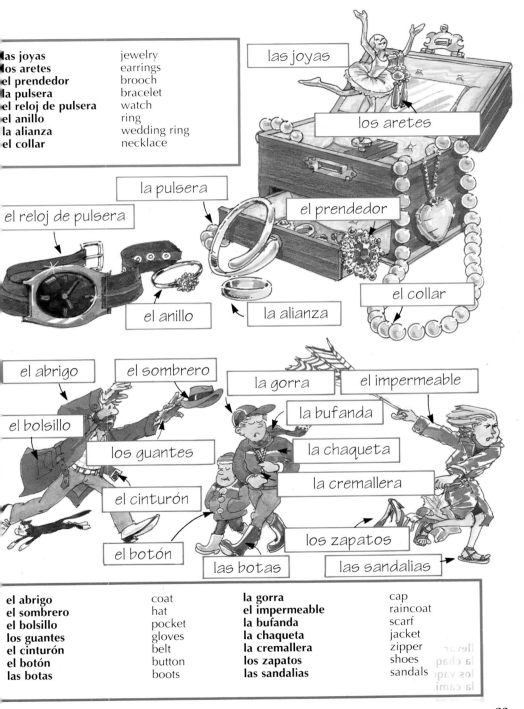

las joyas	jewelry		
los aretes	earrings		
el prendedor	brooch		
la pulsera	bracelet		
el reloj de pulsera	watch		
el anillo	ring		
la alianza	wedding ring		
el collar	necklace		

las joyas

los aretes

la pulsera

el prendedor

el reloj de pulsera

el anillo

la alianza

el collar

el abrigo

el sombrero

la gorra

el impermeable

el bolsillo

la bufanda

los guantes

la chaqueta

el cinturón

la cremallera

el botón

los zapatos

las botas

las sandalias

el abrigo	coat	**la gorra**	cap
el sombrero	hat	**el impermeable**	raincoat
el bolsillo	pocket	**la bufanda**	scarf
los guantes	gloves	**la chaqueta**	jacket
el cinturón	belt	**la cremallera**	zipper
el botón	button	**los zapatos**	shoes
las botas	boots	**las sandalias**	sandals

23

Going to bed

la hora de acostarse — bedtime
encender la luz — to turn on the light
estar cansado(a) — to be tired
ordenar — to tidy up
quitarse la ropa — to get undressed

la hora de acostarse

encender la luz

estar cansada

ordenar

quitarse la ropa

poner el baño

bañarse

la bañera

el tapón

la bata de baño

salpicar

la alfombrita de baño

la báscula

poner el baño — to run a bath
bañarse — to take a bath
la bañera — bathtub
el tapón — plug
la bata de baño — bathrobe
salpicar — to splash
la alfombrita de baño — bathmat
la báscula — scales

24

acostarse

el pijama

el camisón

las zapatillas

acostarse	to go to bed
el pijama	pajamas
el camisón	nightdress
las zapatillas	slippers

la canción de cuna

leer un cuento

la cuna

dormirse

la canción de cuna	lullaby
leer un cuento	to read a story
la cuna	crib
dormirse	to fall asleep

¡Hasta mañana!

¡Que duerman bien!

soñar

roncar

dormir

la almohada

apagar

la lámpara

la sábana

el edredón

la colcha

la mesita de noche

la cama

¡Hasta mañana!	Good night!	el edredón	quilt
¡Que duerman bien! (pl)	Sleep well!	la cama	bed
soñar	to dream	roncar	to snore
dormir	to sleep	la almohada	pillow
apagar	to turn off the light	la sábana	sheet
la lámpara	lamp	la colcha	bedspread
la mesita de noche	bedside table		

25

Eating and drinking

poner la mesa	to set the table
Está listo.	It's ready.
la cafetera	coffee pot
la tetera	teapot
la servilleta	napkin
el vaso	glass
el tazón	bowl
el plato	plate
la taza	cup
el platito	saucer
el mantel	tablecloth
la jarra	pitcher
la cuchara	spoon
el cuchillo	knife
el tenedor	fork

poner la mesa

Está listo.

la cafetera

la tetera

la servilleta

la cuchara

el cuchillo

el tenedor

el vaso

la taza

el platito

el plato

la jarra

el tazón

el mantel

¡Sírvete!

¡Que aproveche!

tener hambre

comer

tener sed

beber

Está muy rico.

haber comido bien

¡Sírvete!	Help yourself.
¡Que aproveche!	Enjoy your meal.
tener sed	to be thirsty
beber	to drink
tener hambre	to be hungry
comer	to eat
Está muy rico.	It tastes good.
haber comido bien	to have eaten well

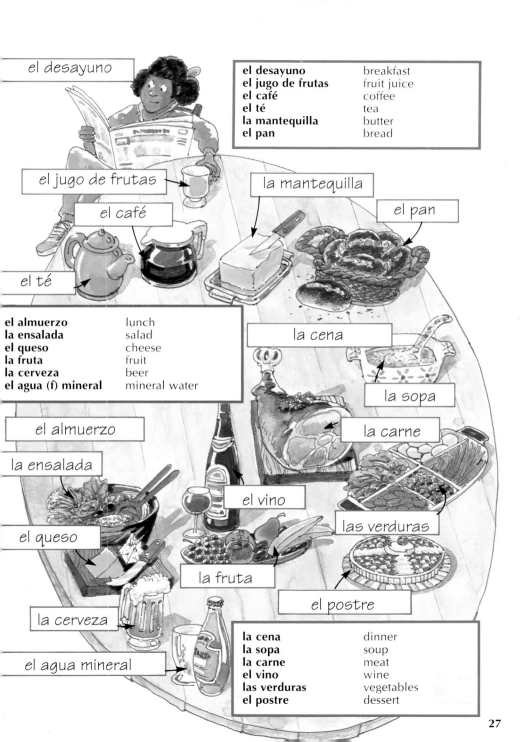

el desayuno

el desayuno	breakfast
el jugo de frutas	fruit juice
el café	coffee
el té	tea
la mantequilla	butter
el pan	bread

el jugo de frutas

la mantequilla

el pan

el café

el té

el almuerzo	lunch
la ensalada	salad
el queso	cheese
la fruta	fruit
la cerveza	beer
el agua (f) mineral	mineral water

la cena

la sopa

el almuerzo

la carne

la ensalada

el vino

las verduras

el queso

la fruta

el postre

la cerveza

el agua mineral

la cena	dinner
la sopa	soup
la carne	meat
el vino	wine
las verduras	vegetables
el postre	dessert

27

Buying food

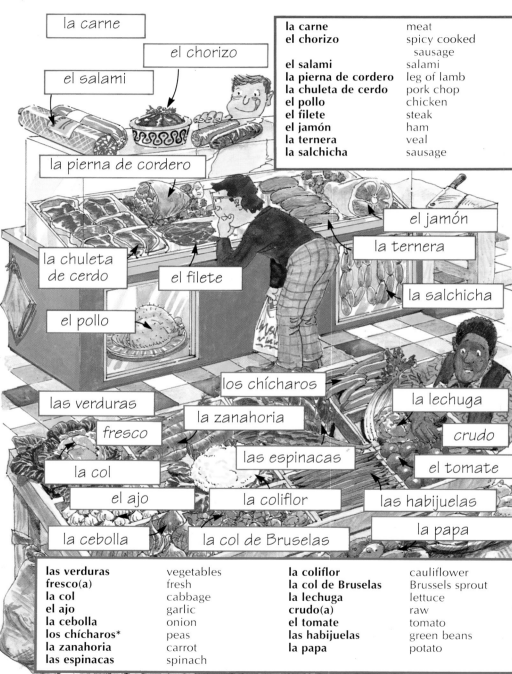

la carne

el chorizo

el salami

la carne	meat
el chorizo	spicy cooked
	sausage
el salami	salami
la pierna de cordero	leg of lamb
la chuleta de cerdo	pork chop
el pollo	chicken
el filete	steak
el jamón	ham
la ternera	veal
la salchicha	sausage

la pierna de cordero

el jamón

la ternera

la chuleta de cerdo

el filete

la salchicha

el pollo

los chícharos

las verduras

la zanahoria

la lechuga

fresco

crudo

la col

las espinacas

el tomate

el ajo

la coliflor

las habijuelas

la cebolla

la col de Bruselas

la papa

las verduras	vegetables	la coliflor	cauliflower
fresco(a)	fresh	la col de Bruselas	Brussels sprout
la col	cabbage	la lechuga	lettuce
el ajo	garlic	crudo(a)	raw
la cebolla	onion	el tomate	tomato
los chícharos*	peas	las habijuelas	green beans
la zanahoria	carrot	la papa	potato
las espinacas	spinach		

*The word for "peas" varies in different parts of Latin America: los chícharos is commonly used in Mexico, but in other countries _____ is more _____

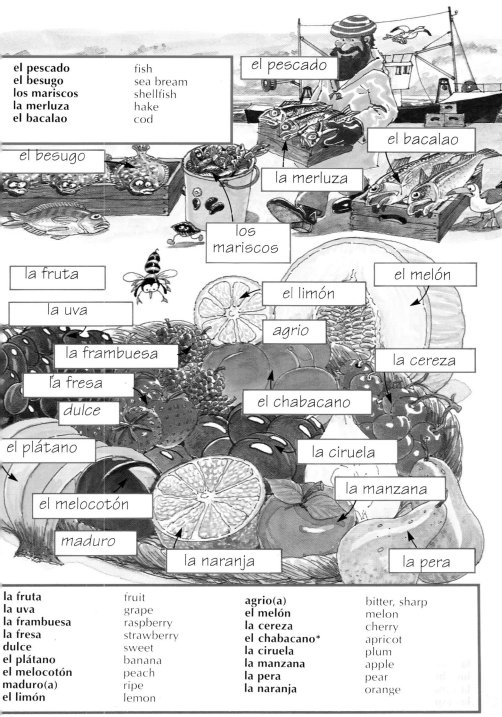

el pescado	fish		
el besugo	sea bream		
los mariscos	shellfish		
la merluza	hake		
el bacalao	cod		

el pescado

el besugo

el bacalao

la merluza

los mariscos

la fruta

el melón

la uva

el limón

la frambuesa

agrio

la cereza

la fresa

el chabacano

dulce

el plátano

la ciruela

la manzana

el melocotón

maduro

la naranja

la pera

la fruta	fruit	agrio(a)	bitter, sharp
la uva	grape	el melón	melon
la frambuesa	raspberry	la cereza	cherry
la fresa	strawberry	el chabacano*	apricot
dulce	sweet	la ciruela	plum
el plátano	banana	la manzana	apple
el melocotón	peach	la pera	pear
maduro(a)	ripe	la naranja	orange
el limón	lemon		

The word for 'apricots' also varies from country to country: **el chabacano** in Mexico, **el albaricoque** or **el damasco** in other countries.

Buying food

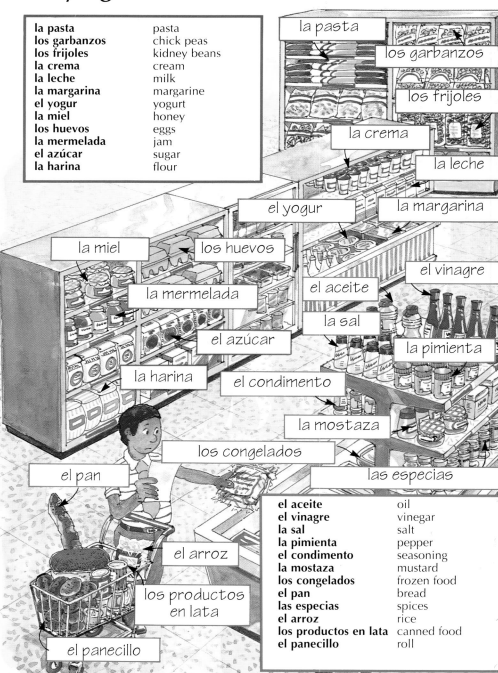

la pasta	pasta
los garbanzos	chick peas
los frijoles	kidney beans
la crema	cream
la leche	milk
la margarina	margarine
el yogur	yogurt
la miel	honey
los huevos	eggs
la mermelada	jam
el azúcar	sugar
la harina	flour

la pasta

los garbanzos

los frijoles

la crema

la leche

el yogur

la margarina

la miel

los huevos

el vinagre

el aceite

la mermelada

la sal

la pimienta

el azúcar

el condimento

la harina

la mostaza

los congelados

las especias

el pan

el arroz

los productos en lata

el panecillo

el aceite	oil
el vinagre	vinegar
la sal	salt
la pimienta	pepper
el condimento	seasoning
la mostaza	mustard
los congelados	frozen food
el pan	bread
las especias	spices
el arroz	rice
los productos en lata	canned food
el panecillo	roll

el chocolate	chocolate
la galletita	cookie
la tarta	tart
el buñuelo	doughnut
el pastel	cake
el helado	ice cream
el pastelillo	pastry, small tart

el chocolate

la galletita

la tarta

el buñuelo

el pastelillo

el pastel

el helado

cocinar

la receta

probar

el sabor

el ingrediente

mezclar

¡Riquísimo!

cocinar	to cook
la receta	recipe
el ingrediente	ingredient
mezclar	to mix
probar	to taste
el sabor	flavor, taste
¡Riquísimo!	Delicious!

Pastimes

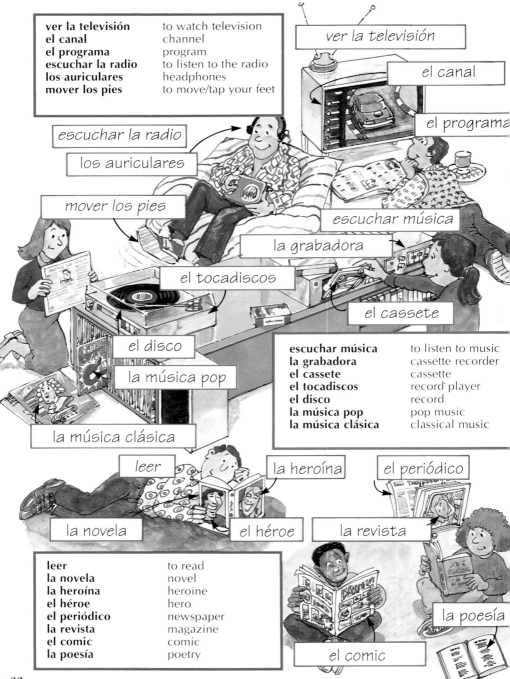

ver la televisión	to watch television
el canal	channel
el programa	program
escuchar la radio	to listen to the radio
los auriculares	headphones
mover los pies	to move/tap your feet

ver la televisión

el canal

el programa

escuchar la radio

los auriculares

mover los pies

escuchar música

la grabadora

el tocadiscos

el cassete

el disco

la música pop

la música clásica

escuchar música	to listen to music
la grabadora	cassette recorder
el cassete	cassette
el tocadiscos	record player
el disco	record
la música pop	pop music
la música clásica	classical music

leer

la heroína

el periódico

la novela

el héroe

la revista

leer	to read
la novela	novel
la heroína	heroine
el héroe	hero
el periódico	newspaper
la revista	magazine
el comic	comic
la poesía	poetry

la poesía

el comic

tejer

las agujas

el patrón

tejer	to knit
las agujas	needles
el patrón	pattern
la lana	wool

la lana

coser

coser	to sew
la tela	fabric
las tijeras	scissors
el hilo	thread
el alfiler	pin
la aguja	needle
la cinta elástica	elastic

la tela

el hilo

la cinta elástica

la aguja

las tijeras

el alfiler

la carpintería

hábil

el martillo

reparar

el tornillo

el destornillador

la sierra

hacer

la carpintería	woodwork
hábil	skillful, good with your hands
la sierra	saw
hacer	to make
el martillo	hammer
reparar	to mend, to repair
el tornillo	screw
el destornillador	screwdriver

Pastimes

la fotografía

tomar una foto

la máquina fotográfica

la fotografía	photography
tomar una foto	to take a photograph
la máquina fotográfica	camera
la máquina de vídeo	video camera
la película	film
la foto	photograph
enfocado	in focus
desenfocado	out of focus

la máquina de vídeo

la foto

enfocado

desenfocado

la película

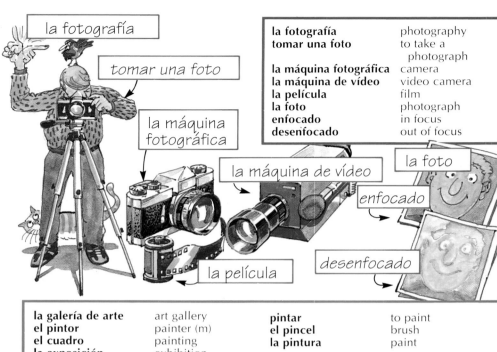

la galería de arte	art gallery	**pintar**	to paint	
el pintor	painter (m)	**el pincel**	brush	
el cuadro	painting	**la pintura**	paint	
la exposición	exhibition			

la galería de arte

el pintor

el cuadro

pintar

la exposición

el pincel

la pintura

ordenar	to sort, to arrange
pegar	to stick
coleccionar estampillas	to collect stamps
la colección	collection

coleccionar estampillas

ordenar

pegar

la colección

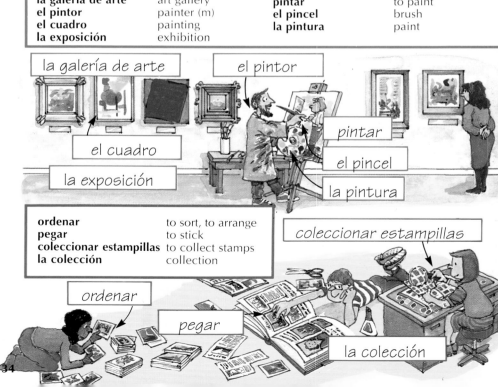

la solista	soloist (f)	tocar los tambores	to play the drums
el instrumento	instrument	tocar la trompeta	to play the trumpet
tocar el violín	to play the violin	tocar el violonchelo	to play the cello
tocar el piano	to play the piano	la orquesta	orchestra
tocar la guitarra	to play the guitar	el director de orquesta	conductor (m)

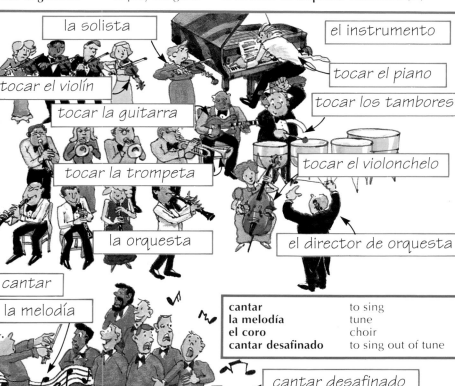

la solista

el instrumento

tocar el violín

tocar el piano

tocar la guitarra

tocar los tambores

tocar la trompeta

tocar el violonchelo

la orquesta

el director de orquesta

cantar

la melodía

cantar	to sing
la melodía	tune
el coro	choir
cantar desafinado	to sing out of tune

cantar desafinado

el coro

los juegos

jugar a las cartas

jugar a las damas

los juegos	games
jugar a las cartas	to play cards
jugar a las damas	to play checkers
jugar al ajedrez	to play chess
los juegos de mesa	board games

los juegos de mesa

jugar al ajedrez

35

Going out

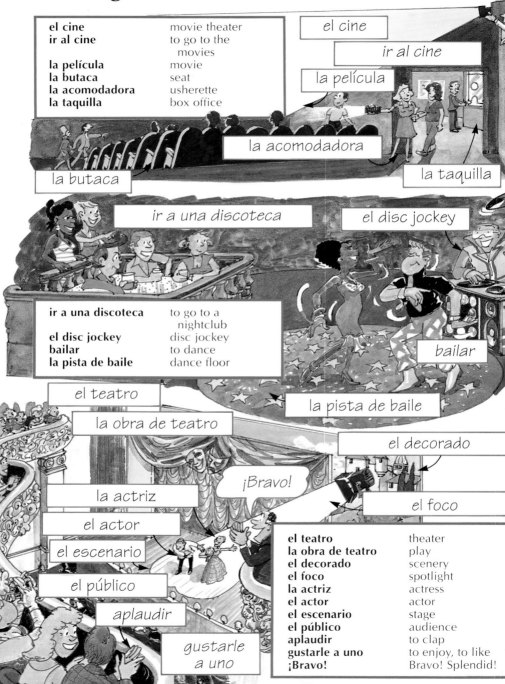

el cine	movie theater
ir al cine	to go to the movies
la película	movie
la butaca	seat
la acomodadora	usherette
la taquilla	box office

el cine

ir al cine

la película

la acomodadora

la butaca

la taquilla

ir a una discoteca

el disc jockey

ir a una discoteca	to go to a nightclub
el disc jockey	disc jockey
bailar	to dance
la pista de baile	dance floor

bailar

el teatro

la obra de teatro

la pista de baile

el decorado

¡Bravo!

la actriz

el foco

el actor

el escenario

el público

aplaudir

gustarle a uno

el teatro	theater
la obra de teatro	play
el decorado	scenery
el foco	spotlight
la actriz	actress
el actor	actor
el escenario	stage
el público	audience
aplaudir	to clap
gustarle a uno	to enjoy, to like
¡Bravo!	Bravo! Splendid!

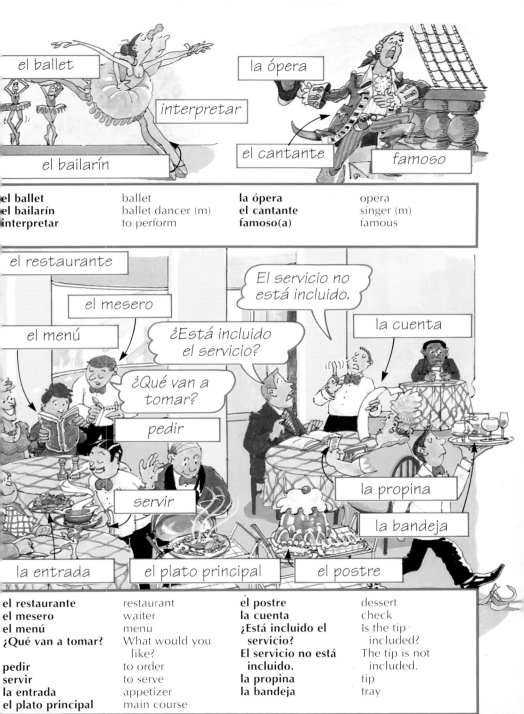

el ballet

la ópera

interpretar

el cantante

famoso

el bailarín

el ballet	ballet	**la ópera**	opera
el bailarín	ballet dancer (m)	**el cantante**	singer (m)
interpretar	to perform	**famoso(a)**	famous

el restaurante

El servicio no está incluido.

el mesero

la cuenta

el menú

¿Está incluido el servicio?

¿Qué van a tomar?

pedir

la propina

servir

la bandeja

la entrada

el plato principal

el postre

el restaurante	restaurant	**el postre**	dessert
el mesero	waiter	**la cuenta**	check
el menú	menu	**¿Está incluido el servicio?**	Is the tip included?
¿Qué van a tomar?	What would you like?	**El servicio no está incluido.**	The tip is not included.
pedir	to order	**la propina**	tip
servir	to serve	**la bandeja**	tray
la entrada	appetizer		
el plato principal	main course		

At the zoo

el zoológico	zoo
el animal	animal
la cebra	zebra
la jirafa	giraffe
el oso blanco	polar bear
el elefante	elephant
la trompa	trunk
el colmillo	tusk
el gorila	gorilla
salvaje	wild
manso(a)	tame
dar de comer	to feed
el guardián	keeper

el zoológico

el animal

la cebra

la jirafa

el oso blanco

el elefante

la trompa

el gorila

salvaje

manso

el colmillo

dar de comer

el guardián

In the park

el parque	park
el estanque	pond
el bote de remos	rowboat
remar	to row
el remo	oar
el picnic	picnic
el banco	bench
descansar	to rest

el parque

el estanque

el bote de remos

remar

el remo

descansar

el picnic

el banco

el mono

el canguro

el avestruz

el camello

la giba

el mono	monkey
el canguro	kangaroo
el avestruz	ostrich
el camello	camel
la giba	hump
el águila (f)	eagle
el pingüino	penguin
el hipopótamo	hippopotamus
la jaula	cage
el león	lion
rugir	to roar
el tigre	tiger
la serpiente	snake

la jaula

el león

el águila

rugir

el pingüino

el tigre

el hipopótamo

la serpiente

el guardián

el columpio

el guardián	ranger
el columpio	swing
vigilar	to keep an eye on
trepar	to climb
cavar	to dig
el tobogán	slide
el carrusel	merry-go-round
colgarse de	to hang on to

vigilar

trepar

el tobogán

el carrusel

cavar

colgarse de

In the city

la capital

las afueras

la ciudad

el puente

el rascacielos

el río

la catedral

el distrito

el edificio

la iglesia

el cementerio

la capital	capital town or city
las afueras	suburbs
la ciudad	town
el rascacielos	skyscraper
la catedral	cathedral
el río	river
el puente	bridge
el distrito	district
el edificio	building
la iglesia	church
el cementerio	cemetery

la estación
de bomberos

el municipio

la comisaría

el bloque de oficinas

el camión de bomberos

el coche
de policía

la fábrica

la biblioteca

la estación de bomberos	fire station	**el bloque de oficinas**	office building
el camión de bomberos	fire engine	**la comisaría**	police station
la fábrica	factory	**el coche de policía**	police car
el municipio	town hall	**la biblioteca**	library

el centro	downtown
la calle	street
estrecho(a)	narrow
ancho(a)	broad
la esquina	corner
cruzar la calle	to cross the street
el paso de peatones	pedestrian crossing
el peatón	pedestrian
la plaza	square
la estatua	statue
el poste de la luz	street light
el mercado	market
el paso subterráneo	subway

el quiosco de periódicos	newspaper stand
la paloma	pigeon
el grupo de gente	crowd
animado	bustling
el basurero	trash bin
la acera	sidewalk
apurarse	to hurry
el anuncio	advertisement

el centro

la calle

ancha

estrecha

la esquina

cruzar la calle

el paso de peatones

el peatón

la plaza

la estatua

el mercado

el poste de la luz

el paso subterráneo

el quiosco de periódicos

la paloma

el grupo de gente

animado

el basurero

el anuncio

la acera

apurarse

Shopping

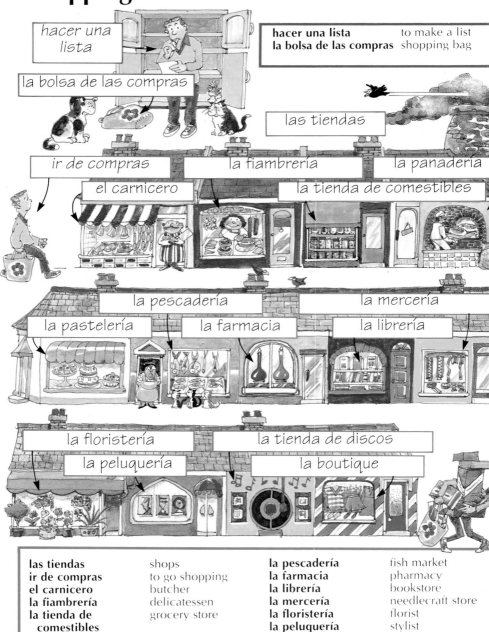

hacer una lista

la bolsa de las compras

| hacer una lista | to make a list |
| la bolsa de las compras | shopping bag |

las tiendas

ir de compras

la fiambrería

la panadería

el carnicero

la tienda de comestibles

la pescadería

la mercería

la pastelería

la farmacia

la librería

la floristería

la tienda de discos

la peluquería

la boutique

las tiendas	shops	la pescadería	fish market
ir de compras	to go shopping	la farmacia	pharmacy
el carnicero	butcher	la librería	bookstore
la fiambrería	delicatessen	la mercería	needlecraft store
la tienda de comestibles	grocery store	la floristería	florist
		la peluquería	stylist
la panadería	bakery	la tienda de discos	music store
la pastelería	cake store	la boutique	boutique

hacer las compras

el puesto

hacer cola

hacer las compras	to do the shopping
el puesto	market stall
hacer cola	to stand in line

Un kilo de...

Medio kilo de...

Son...

¿Cuánto es todo?

pesar

¿Cuánto es todo?	How much do I owe you?
Son...	That will be...
pesar	to weigh
Un kilo de...	A kilo of...
Medio kilo de...	Half a kilo of...

el altoparlante

ir al supermercado

la cesta

el mostrador

la lata

la nave

el paquete

el carrito

la botella

la entrada

la salida

la caja

la bolsa

la cajera

ir al supermercado	to go to the supermarket
la cesta	basket
el carrito	cart
el altoparlante	loudspeaker, intercom
el mostrador	counter
la nave	aisle
la lata	can
el paquete	packet
la botella	bottle
la entrada	entrance
la salida	exit
la caja	checkout
la bolsa	grocery bag
la cajera	cashier (f)

Shopping

ir a mirar vidrieras	to go window-shopping	**saldos (m. pl)**	sale
la vidriera	store window	**una ganga (f)**	a bargain
Está a buen precio.	It's a good value.	**la clienta**	customer (f)
Es bastante caro.	It's rather expensive.	**comprar**	to buy
		la vendedora	sales assistant (f)
		vender	to sell

ir a mirar vidrieras

la vidriera

Está a buen precio.

Es bastante caro.

la clienta

comprar

la vendedora

vender

SALDOS

una ganga

gastar dinero

el precio

el recibo

¿Qué desea?

Querría...

¿Qué talla es esto?

chico

mediano

grande

¿Cuánto cuesta...?

Cuesta...

gastar dinero	to spend money	**chico**	small
el precio	price	**mediano**	medium
el recibo	receipt	**grande**	large
¿Qué desea?	Can I help you?	**¿Cuánto cuesta...?**	How much is...?
Querría...	I'd like...	**Cuesta...**	It costs...
¿Qué talla es esto?	What size is this?		

la librería y	bookstore and	**la postal**	postcard
papelería	stationer's	**el bolígrafo**	ball point pen
el libro	book	**el lápiz**	pencil
la edición de bolsillo	paperback	**el papel de escribir**	writing paper
el sobre	envelope		

la librería y papelería

el sobre

la postal

el libro

el bolígrafo

el lápiz

la edición de bolsillo

el papel de escribir

los grandes almacenes

el departamento

el ascensor

la escalera automática

JUGUETES

ARTÍCULOS DE DEPORTE

MUEBLES

ROPA

los grandes almacenes	department store	**juguetes (m. pl)**	toys
el departamento	department	**muebles (m. pl)**	furniture
la escalera automática	escalator	**artículos de deporte (m. pl)**	sports equipment
el ascensor	elevator	**ropa (f)**	clothes, clothing

At the post office and bank

la oficina de correos	post office	el telegrama	telegram
el buzón	mailbox	**el formulario**	form
echar al correo	to mail	**el sello**	stamp
la carta	letter	**por avión**	airmail
el paquete	parcel	**la dirección**	address
las horas de recogida	collection times	**el código postal**	zip code
mandar	to send		

el cartero	mailman
el correo	mail
entregar	to deliver

46

el banco

el cajero

el dinero

¿Tiene cambio?

cambiar dinero

la moneda

el tipo de cambio

el billete

la tarjeta de crédito

el gerente del banco

meter dinero en el banco

sacar dinero del banco

la billetera

la chequera

hacer un cheque

el monedero

la cartera

el banco	bank	la tarjeta de crédito	credit card
el dinero	money	meter dinero en el banco	to put money in the bank
cambiar dinero	to exchange money	sacar dinero del banco	to take money out of the bank
el tipo de cambio	exchange rate		
el gerente del banco	bank manager		
el cajero	cashier (m)	la chequera	check book
¿Tiene cambio?	Do you have any change?	hacer un cheque	to write a check
		la billetera	billfold
la moneda	coin	el monedero	coin purse
el billete	bill	la cartera	purse

Phonecalls and letters

hacer una llamada	to make a telephone call	**la guía telefónica**	telephone directory
el teléfono	telephone	**sonar**	to ring
el auricular	receiver	**atender el teléfono**	to answer the telephone
descolgar	to pick up the receiver	**¡Hola!**	Hello!
marcar el número	to dial the number	**¿Quién habla?**	Who's speaking?
el número de teléfono	telephone number	**Soy Juanita.**	It's Juanita.
		Te llamo más tarde.	I'll call you back.
el código regional	area code	**¡Adiós!**	Goodbye.
		colgar	to hang up

la cabina de teléfono	payphone
la emergencia	emergency
la llamada de emergencia	911 call

escribir una carta

Muy señor mío:/ Estimada señora:

Gracias por su carta del...

Adjunto...

Le saluda atentamente,

...a vuelta de correo.

12 de marzo de 1997

escribir una carta	to write a letter	Adjunto...	I enclose...
Muy señor mío:/ Estimada señora:	Dear Sir/Madam,	...a vuelta de correo	return mail
Gracias por su carta del...	Thank you for your letter of...	Le saluda atentamente,	Yours faithfully,

abrir una carta

Querida Juanita:

Me encantó tener noticias tuyas.

Te mando por separado...

Un abrazo de...

9 de enero de 1999

abrir una carta	to open a letter	Te mando por separado...	I am sending... separately.
Querida Juanita:	Dear Juanita	Un abrazo de...	Love from...
Me encantó tener noticias tuyas.	It was lovely to hear from you.		

mandar una postal

Pasándolo muy bien.

Deseando verte pronto.

mandar un telegrama

MENSAJE URGENTE

PUNTO LLAMA

A CASA

mandar una postal	to send a postcard	mandar un telegrama	to send a telegram
Pasándolo muy bien.	Having a lovely time.	Mensaje urgente punto llama a casa	Urgent message stop telephone home
Deseando verte pronto.	Look forward to seeing you soon.		

49

Out and about

ir a pie

correr

¿Por dónde está...?

la señal

preguntar el camino

el mapa

¿A qué distancia está...?

el cochecito

ir a pie	to walk	**el mapa**	map
correr	to run	**la señal**	sign
el cochecito	stroller	**¿A qué distancia**	How far is...?
¿Por dónde está...?	Which way is...?	**está...?**	
preguntar el camino	to ask the way		

tomar el camión

el pasajero

bajarse

el boleto

la estación de metro

subirse

el camión

el metro

la parada de camiones

tomar el camión*	to take the bus	**el camión**	bus
el pasajero	passenger (m)	**la parada de camiones**	bus stop
bajarse	to get off	**la estación de metro**	subway station
subirse	to get on	**el metro**	subway
el boleto	ticket		

*The word for bus varies in different parts of Latin America

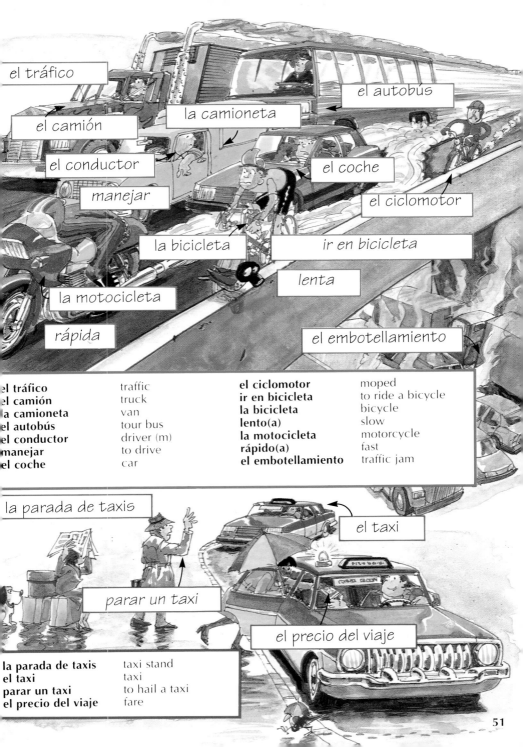

el tráfico

el camión

la camioneta

el autobús

el conductor

el coche

manejar

el ciclomotor

la bicicleta

ir en bicicleta

lenta

la motocicleta

rápida

el embotellamiento

el tráfico	traffic	el ciclomotor	moped
el camión	truck	ir en bicicleta	to ride a bicycle
la camioneta	van	la bicicleta	bicycle
el autobús	tour bus	lento(a)	slow
el conductor	driver (m)	la motocicleta	motorcycle
manejar	to drive	rápido(a)	fast
el coche	car	el embotellamiento	traffic jam

la parada de taxis

el taxi

parar un taxi

el precio del viaje

la parada de taxis	taxi stand
el taxi	taxi
parar un taxi	to hail a taxi
el precio del viaje	fare

51

Driving

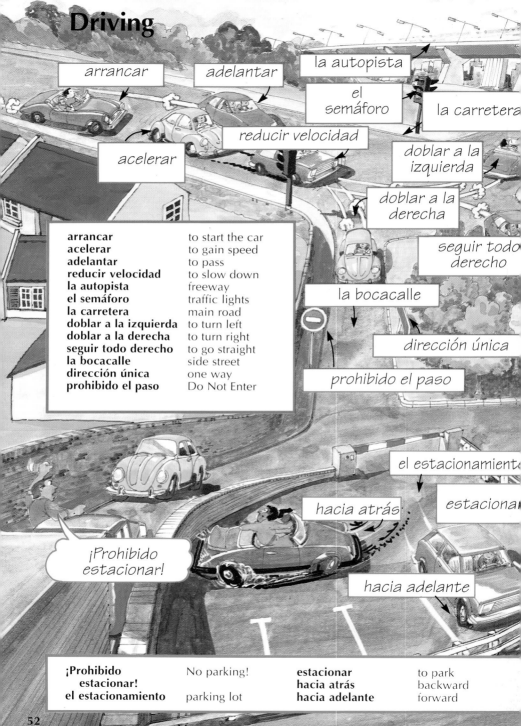

arrancar

adelantar

la autopista

el semáforo

la carretera

reducir velocidad

acelerar

doblar a la izquierda

doblar a la derecha

seguir todo derecho

arrancar	to start the car
acelerar	to gain speed
adelantar	to pass
reducir velocidad	to slow down
la autopista	freeway
el semáforo	traffic lights
la carretera	main road
doblar a la izquierda	to turn left
doblar a la derecha	to turn right
seguir todo derecho	to go straight
la bocacalle	side street
dirección única	one way
prohibido el paso	Do Not Enter

la bocacalle

dirección única

prohibido el paso

el estacionamiento

estaciona

hacia atrás

¡Prohibido estacionar!

hacia adelante

¡Prohibido estacionar!	No parking!	**estacionar**	to park	
		hacia atrás	backward	
el estacionamiento	parking lot	**hacia adelante**	forward	

52

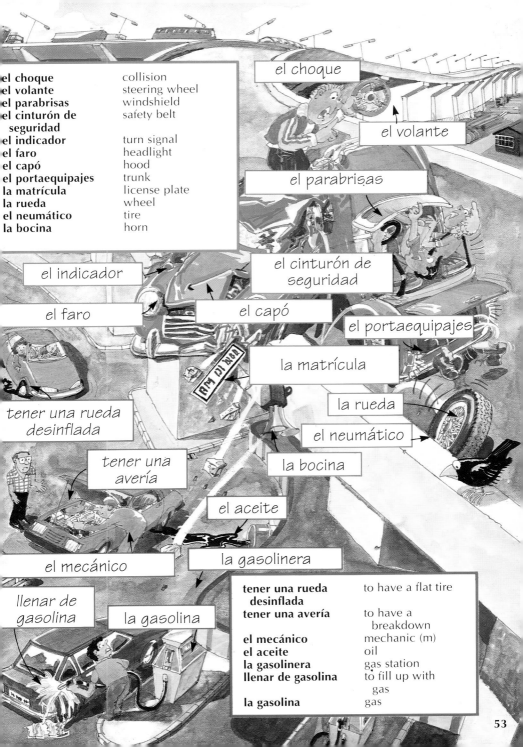

el choque	collision
el volante	steering wheel
el parabrisas	windshield
el cinturón de seguridad	safety belt
el indicador	turn signal
el faro	headlight
el capó	hood
el portaequipajes	trunk
la matrícula	license plate
la rueda	wheel
el neumático	tire
la bocina	horn

el choque

el volante

el parabrisas

el cinturón de seguridad

el indicador

el faro

el capó

el portaequipajes

la matrícula

la rueda

el neumático

tener una rueda desinflada

tener una avería

la bocina

el aceite

el mecánico

la gasolinera

llenar de gasolina

la gasolina

tener una rueda desinflada	to have a flat tire
tener una avería	to have a breakdown
el mecánico	mechanic (m)
el aceite	oil
la gasolinera	gas station
llenar de gasolina	to fill up with gas
la gasolina	gas

Traveling by train

la estación

la consigna

el mozo

el revisor

la sala de espera

la barrera

el viajero

el horario

la ventanilla

El tren para...

el boleto

El tren desde...

el boleto de ida y vuelta

el abono

la máquina de boletos

reservar un asiento

el boleto urbano

la estación	station	**El tren desde...**	The train from...
el mozo	porter	**la ventanilla**	ticket office
la consigna	baggage room	**el boleto**	ticket
el revisor	ticket collector	**el boleto de ida**	round trip ticket
la sala de espera	waiting room	**y vuelta**	
la barrera	barrier	**el abono**	season ticket
el viajero	traveler (m)	**la máquina de boletos**	ticket machine
el horario	timetable	**el boleto urbano**	local ticket (in city)
El tren para...	The train to...	**reservar un asiento**	to reserve a seat

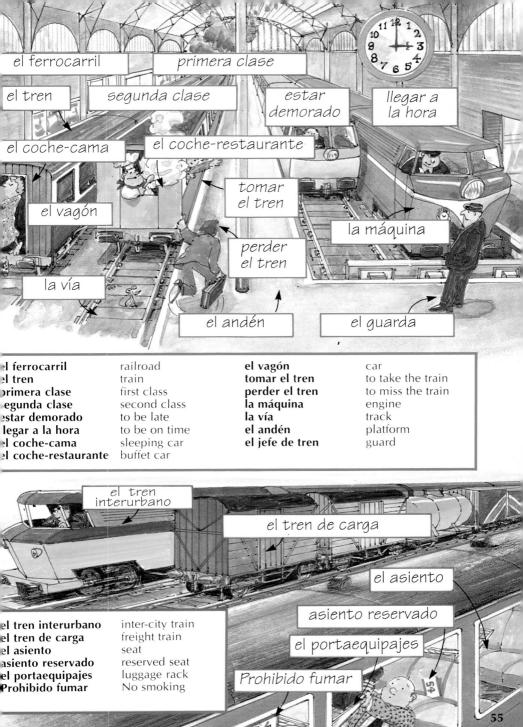

el ferrocarril

primera clase

el tren

segunda clase

estar demorado

llegar a la hora

el coche-cama

el coche-restaurante

tomar el tren

la máquina

el vagón

perder el tren

la vía

el andén

el guarda

el ferrocarril	railroad	**el vagón**	car
el tren	train	**tomar el tren**	to take the train
primera clase	first class	**perder el tren**	to miss the train
segunda clase	second class	**la máquina**	engine
estar demorado	to be late	**la vía**	track
llegar a la hora	to be on time	**el andén**	platform
el coche-cama	sleeping car	**el jefe de tren**	guard
el coche-restaurante	buffet car		

el tren interurbano

el tren de carga

el asiento

asiento reservado

el portaequipajes

Prohibido fumar

el tren interurbano	inter-city train
el tren de carga	freight train
el asiento	seat
asiento reservado	reserved seat
el portaequipajes	luggage rack
Prohibido fumar	No smoking

55

Traveling by plane and boat

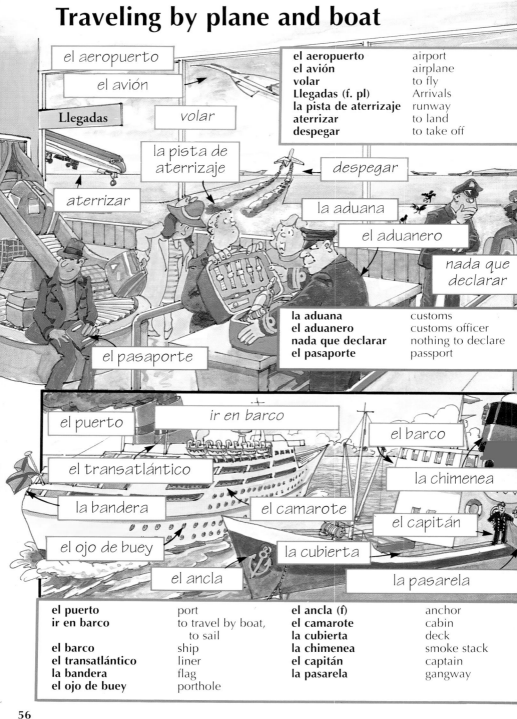

el aeropuerto

el avión

Llegadas

volar

la pista de aterrizaje

aterrizar

despegar

la aduana

el aduanero

nada que declarar

el pasaporte

el aeropuerto	airport
el avión	airplane
volar	to fly
Llegadas (f. pl)	Arrivals
la pista de aterrizaje	runway
aterrizar	to land
despegar	to take off

la aduana	customs
el aduanero	customs officer
nada que declarar	nothing to declare
el pasaporte	passport

el puerto

ir en barco

el barco

el transatlántico

la chimenea

la bandera

el camarote

el capitán

el ojo de buey

la cubierta

el ancla

la pasarela

el puerto	port
ir en barco	to travel by boat, to sail
el barco	ship
el transatlántico	liner
la bandera	flag
el ojo de buey	porthole

el ancla (f)	anchor
el camarote	cabin
la cubierta	deck
la chimenea	smoke stack
el capitán	captain
la pasarela	gangway

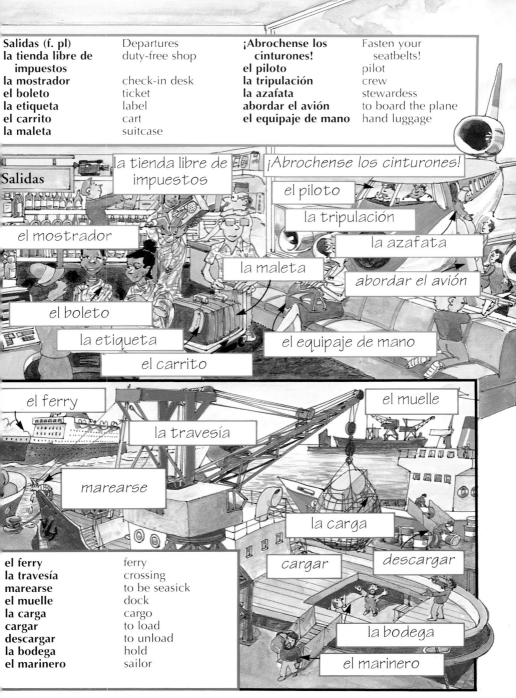

Salidas (f. pl)	Departures
la tienda libre de impuestos	duty-free shop
la mostrador	check-in desk
el boleto	ticket
la etiqueta	label
el carrito	cart
la maleta	suitcase

¡Abrochense los cinturones!	Fasten your seatbelts!
el piloto	pilot
la tripulación	crew
la azafata	stewardess
abordar el avión	to board the plane
el equipaje de mano	hand luggage

Salidas

la tienda libre de impuestos

¡Abrochense los cinturones!

el piloto

la tripulación

el mostrador

la azafata

la maleta

abordar el avión

el boleto

la etiqueta

el equipaje de mano

el carrito

el ferry

el muelle

la travesía

marearse

la carga

cargar

descargar

la bodega

el marinero

el ferry	ferry
la travesía	crossing
marearse	to be seasick
el muelle	dock
la carga	cargo
cargar	to load
descargar	to unload
la bodega	hold
el marinero	sailor

57

On vacation

la turista

ir de vacaciones

hacer la maleta

ir de vacaciones	to go on vacation
hacer la maleta	to pack
la crema bronceadora	suntan lotion
las gafas de sol	sunglasses
la turista	tourist (f)
visitar los lugares de interés	to sightsee

la crema bronceadora

las gafas de sol

visitar los lugares de interés

el hotel

quedarse en un hotel

la recepción

el conserje

con ducha

la habitación individual

con balcón

la habitación doble

reservar una habitación

la pensión

estar completo

el hotel	hotel	**reservar una habitación**	to reserve a room
quedarse en un hotel	to stay in a hotel	**estar completo**	to be fully booked
la recepción	reception	**con ducha**	with shower
el conserje	porter	**con balcón**	with balcony
la habitación individual	single room	**la pensión**	guest house, boarding house
la habitación doble	double room		

en la playa

en la playa	on/at the beach
la gaviota	seagull
el vigilante de playa	lifeguard
la ola	wave
la lancha motora	powerboat
hacer esquí acuático	to waterski
hacer windsurf	to windsurf
nadar	to swim, to take a swim
chapotear	to paddle
el mar	sea
la arena	sand
la playa	beach

la gaviota

el vigilante de playa

la ola

la lancha motora

hacer esquí acuático

hacer windsurf

nadar

chapotear

el mar

la arena

la playa

tomar sol

bronceado

la sombrilla

el castillo de arena

el baldecito

la pala

tomar sol	to sunbathe
bronceado (a)	tanned
la sombrilla	beach umbrella
el castillo de arena	sandcastle
el baldecito	bucket
la pala	spade

el charco

las algas marinas

el cangrejo

las conchitas

el charco	pool
las algas marinas	seaweed
el cangrejo	crab
las conchitas	shells

59

On vacation

hacer alpinismo	to go mountain climbing
la montaña	mountain
la cima	summit
la vista	view
empinado (a)	steep
escalar	to climb
el alpinista	climber (m)
la mochila	backpack

esquiar

el centro de esquí

la cima

hacer alpinismo

la telesilla

la montaña

la vista

escalar

empinado

el alpinista

el instructor de esquí

la mochila

la pista

el trineo

el bastón de esquí

las botas de esquí

los esquís

esquiar	to ski
el centro de esquí	ski resort
la telesilla	ski lift
el instructor de esquí	ski instructor (m)
la pista	ski slope, ski run
el trineo	toboggan
el bastón de esquí	ski pole
las botas de esquí	ski boots
los esquís	skis

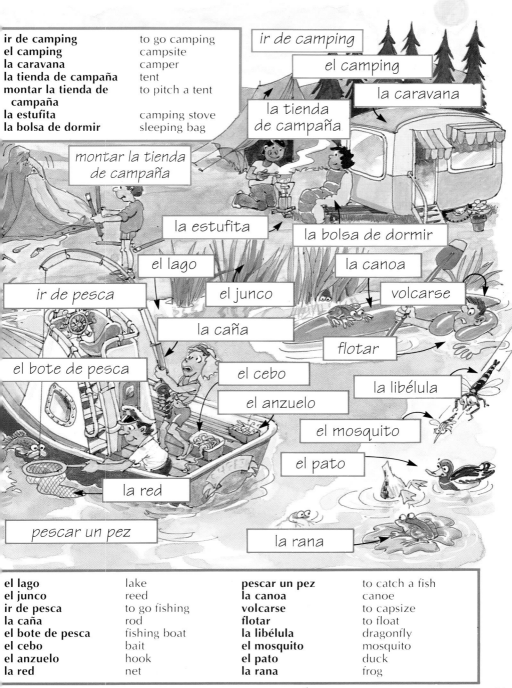

ir de camping	to go camping		
el camping	campsite		
la caravana	camper		
la tienda de campaña	tent		
montar la tienda de campaña	to pitch a tent		
la estufita	camping stove		
la bolsa de dormir	sleeping bag		

ir de camping

el camping

la caravana

la tienda de campaña

montar la tienda de campaña

la estufita

la bolsa de dormir

el lago

la canoa

ir de pesca

el junco

volcarse

la caña

flotar

el bote de pesca

el cebo

la libélula

el anzuelo

el mosquito

el pato

la red

pescar un pez

la rana

el lago	lake	**pescar un pez**	to catch a fish
el junco	reed	**la canoa**	canoe
ir de pesca	to go fishing	**volcarse**	to capsize
la caña	rod	**flotar**	to float
el bote de pesca	fishing boat	**la libélula**	dragonfly
el cebo	bait	**el mosquito**	mosquito
el anzuelo	hook	**el pato**	duck
la red	net	**la rana**	frog

In the countryside

el pueblo

el paisaje

tranquilo

el campo

la cabaña

dar un paseo

el pueblo	village
el paisaje	landscape
tranquilo(a)	peaceful
el campo	countryside
la cabaña	cottage
dar un paseo	to go for a walk

el camino

el prado

el arroyo

el conejo

el camino	path
el arroyo	stream
el prado	meadow
el conejo	rabbit
el topo	mole
subirse a un árbol	to climb a tree
las flores silvestres	wild flowers
recoger flores	to pick flowers
un ramo de flores	a bunch of flowers
la margarita	daisy
la amapola	poppy

el topo

subirse a un árbol

las flores silvestres

recoger flores

un ramo de flores

la margarita

la amapola

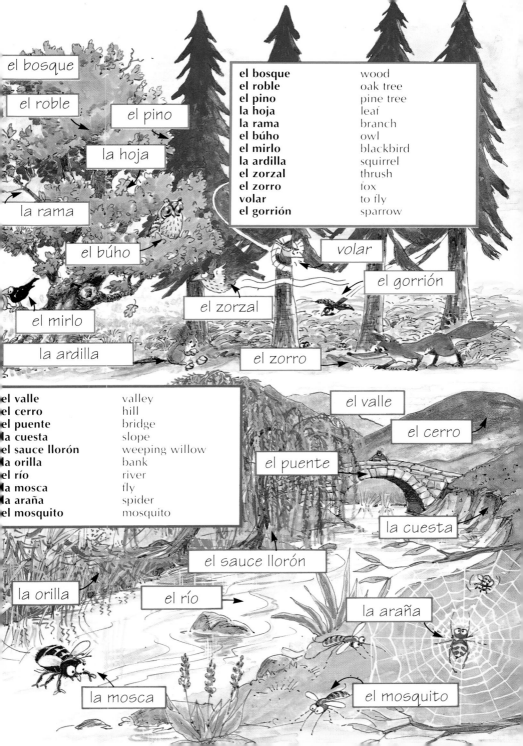

el bosque

el roble

el pino

la hoja

la rama

el bosque	wood
el roble	oak tree
el pino	pine tree
la hoja	leaf
la rama	branch
el búho	owl
el mirlo	blackbird
la ardilla	squirrel
el zorzal	thrush
el zorro	fox
volar	to fly
el gorrión	sparrow

el búho

volar

el gorrión

el zorzal

el mirlo

la ardilla

el zorro

el valle	valley
el cerro	hill
el puente	bridge
la cuesta	slope
el sauce llorón	weeping willow
la orilla	bank
el río	river
la mosca	fly
la araña	spider
el mosquito	mosquito

el valle

el cerro

el puente

la cuesta

el sauce llorón

la orilla

el río

la araña

la mosca

el mosquito

On the farm

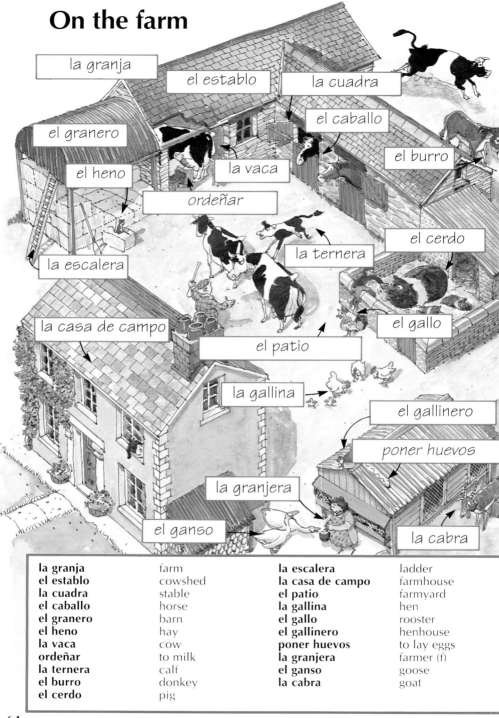

la granja

el establo

la cuadra

el caballo

el granero

el burro

el heno

la vaca

ordeñar

el cerdo

la ternera

la escalera

la casa de campo

el gallo

el patio

la gallina

el gallinero

poner huevos

la granjera

el ganso

la cabra

la granja	farm	**la escalera**	ladder
el establo	cowshed	**la casa de campo**	farmhouse
la cuadra	stable	**el patio**	farmyard
el caballo	horse	**la gallina**	hen
el granero	barn	**el gallo**	rooster
el heno	hay	**el gallinero**	henhouse
la vaca	cow	**poner huevos**	to lay eggs
ordeñar	to milk	**la granjera**	farmer (f)
la ternera	calf	**el ganso**	goose
el burro	donkey	**la cabra**	goat
el cerdo	pig		

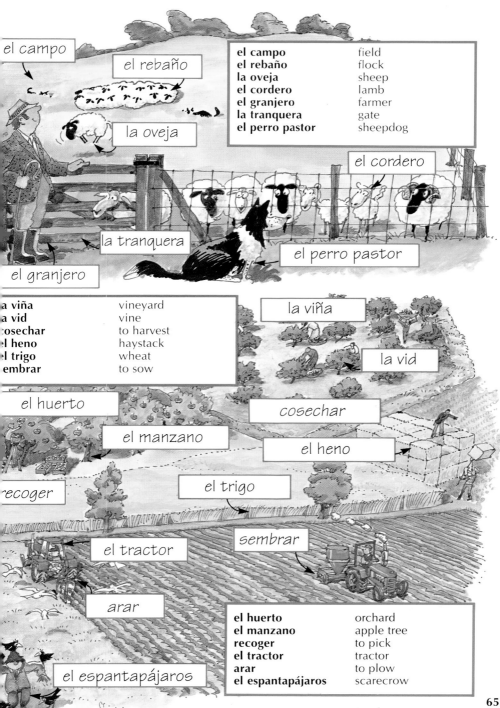

el campo

el rebaño

la oveja

el campo	field
el rebaño	flock
la oveja	sheep
el cordero	lamb
el granjero	farmer
la tranquera	gate
el perro pastor	sheepdog

el cordero

la tranquera

el perro pastor

el granjero

la viña	vineyard
la vid	vine
cosechar	to harvest
el heno	haystack
el trigo	wheat
sembrar	to sow

la viña

la vid

el huerto

cosechar

el manzano

el heno

recoger

el trigo

sembrar

el tractor

arar

el espantapájaros

el huerto	orchard
el manzano	apple tree
recoger	to pick
el tractor	tractor
arar	to plow
el espantapájaros	scarecrow

At work

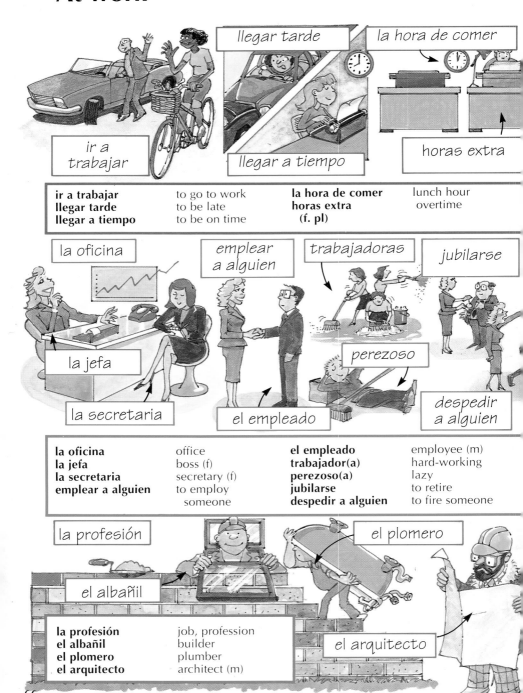

llegar tarde

la hora de comer

ir a trabajar

llegar a tiempo

horas extra

ir a trabajar	to go to work	la hora de comer	lunch hour
llegar tarde	to be late	horas extra (f. pl)	overtime
llegar a tiempo	to be on time		

la oficina

emplear a alguien

trabajadoras

jubilarse

la jefa

perezoso

la secretaria

el empleado

despedir a alguien

la oficina	office	el empleado	employee (m)
la jefa	boss (f)	trabajador(a)	hard-working
la secretaria	secretary (f)	perezoso(a)	lazy
emplear a alguien	to employ someone	jubilarse	to retire
		despedir a alguien	to fire someone

la profesión

el plomero

el albañil

el arquitecto

la profesión	job, profession
el albañil	builder
el plomero	plumber
el arquitecto	architect (m)

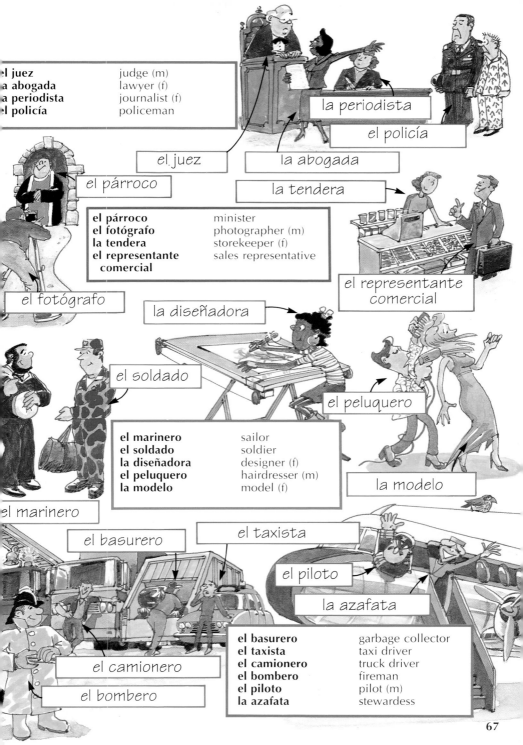

el juez	judge (m)
a abogada	lawyer (f)
a periodista	journalist (f)
l policía	policeman

la periodista

el policía

el juez

la abogada

el párroco

la tendera

el párroco	minister
el fotógrafo	photographer (m)
la tendera	storekeeper (f)
el representante comercial	sales representative

el representante comercial

el fotógrafo

la diseñadora

el soldado

el peluquero

el marinero	sailor
el soldado	soldier
la diseñadora	designer (f)
el peluquero	hairdresser (m)
la modelo	model (f)

la modelo

el marinero

el basurero

el taxista

el piloto

la azafata

el basurero	garbage collector
el taxista	taxi driver
el camionero	truck driver
el bombero	fireman
el piloto	pilot (m)
la azafata	stewardess

el camionero

el bombero

Illness and health

sentirse mal		la receta		sentirse mejor
tomar la temperatura			curar	
el termómetro				
tener fiebre				
la médica		la pastilla		sano

sentirse mal	to feel ill	la médica	doctor (f)
tomar la temperatura	to take someone's temperature	la receta	prescription
el termómetro	thermometer	curar	to cure
tener fiebre	to have a temperature	la pastilla	pill
		sentirse mejor	to feel better
		sano(a)	healthy

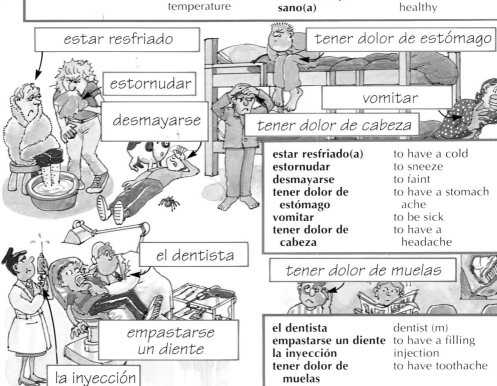

estar resfriado		tener dolor de estómago
estornudar		vomitar
desmayarse		tener dolor de cabeza

estar resfriado(a)	to have a cold
estornudar	to sneeze
desmayarse	to faint
tener dolor de estómago	to have a stomach ache
vomitar	to be sick
tener dolor de cabeza	to have a headache

el dentista	tener dolor de muelas
empastarse un diente	
la inyección	

el dentista	dentist (m)
empastarse un diente	to have a filling
la inyección	injection
tener dolor de muelas	to have toothache

el hospital

urgencias

el moretón

la quemadura

dislocarse
la muñeca

romperse
la pierna

la cortadura

la curita

la venda

l hospital	hospital	**la quemadura**	burn
rgencias	emergency room	**dislocarse la muñeca**	to sprain your
omperse la pierna	to break your leg		wrist
l moretón	bruise	**la curita**	adhesive bandage
a cortadura	cut	**la venda**	bandage

la ambulancia

tomar el pulso

el paciente

la camilla

la ambulancia	ambulance
tomar el pulso	to take someone's
	pulse
la camilla	stretcher
el paciente	patient (m)

el quirófano

la operación

la enfermera

el cirujano

el quirófano	operating room
el cirujano	surgeon (m)
la operación	operation
la enfermera	nurse (f)

69

School and education

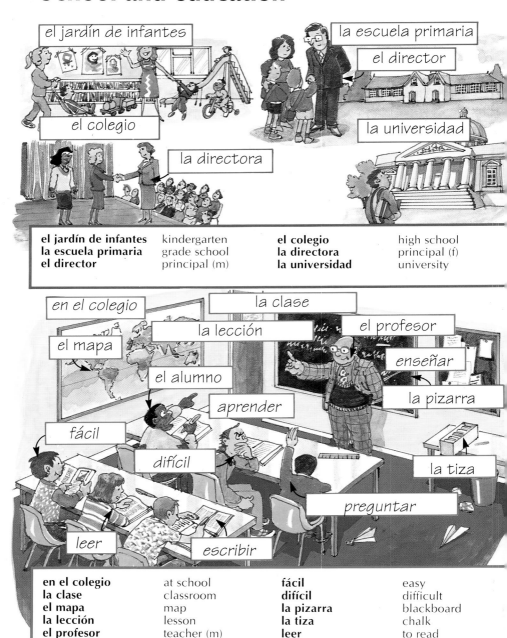

el jardín de infantes

el colegio

la escuela primaria

el director

la directora

la universidad

el jardín de infantes	kindergarten	**el colegio**	high school
la escuela primaria	grade school	**la directora**	principal (f)
el director	principal (m)	**la universidad**	university

en el colegio

la clase

la lección

el profesor

el mapa

enseñar

el alumno

la pizarra

aprender

fácil

difícil

la tiza

preguntar

leer

escribir

en el colegio	at school	**fácil**	easy
la clase	classroom	**difícil**	difficult
el mapa	map	**la pizarra**	blackboard
la lección	lesson	**la tiza**	chalk
el profesor	teacher (m)	**leer**	to read
enseñar	to teach	**escribir**	to write
el alumno	pupil (m)	**preguntar**	to ask a question
aprender	to learn		

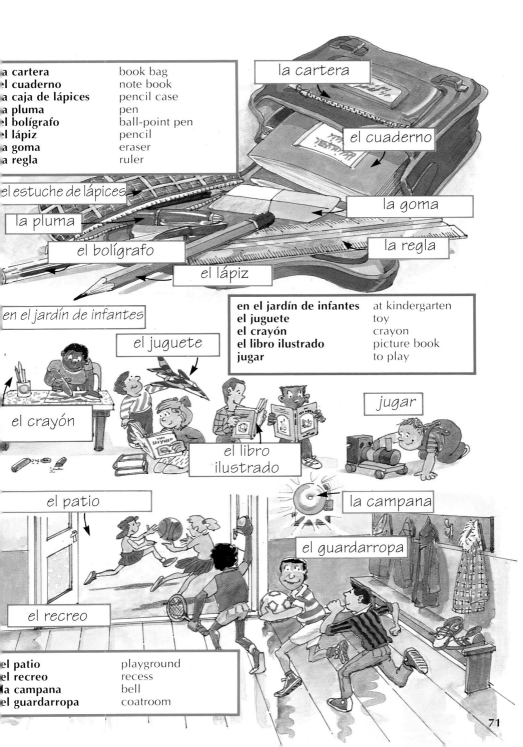

la cartera	book bag
el cuaderno	note book
la caja de lápices	pencil case
la pluma	pen
el bolígrafo	ball-point pen
el lápiz	pencil
la goma	eraser
la regla	ruler

la cartera

el cuaderno

el estuche de lápices

la goma

la pluma

el bolígrafo

la regla

el lápiz

en el jardín de infantes

en el jardín de infantes	at kindergarten
el juguete	toy
el crayón	crayon
el libro ilustrado	picture book
jugar	to play

el juguete

jugar

el crayón

el libro ilustrado

el patio

la campana

el guardarropa

el recreo

el patio	playground
el recreo	recess
la campana	bell
el guardarropa	coatroom

71

School and education

el curso

el horario

la materia

el principio de curso

el español

las matemáticas

la física

el francés

la química

el inglés

la biología

el alemán

la historia

la geografía

la música

el fin de curso

la computación

la gimnasia

el curso	course, academic year	**el alemán**	German
el principio de curso	beginning academic year	**las matemáticas**	math
		la física	physics
el fin de curso	end of year	**la química**	chemistry
el horario	timetable	**la biología**	biology
la materia	subject	**la historia**	history
el español	Spanish	**la geografía**	geography
el francés	French	**la música**	music
el inglés	English	**la computación**	computer studies
		la gimnasia	PE

A B C CH D E F G H I J K L LL M N Ñ O P Q R S T U V W X Y Z

la letra

el alfabeto

la gramática

la ortografía

la mayúscula

la palabra

la frase

el punto

la letra	letter
el alfabeto	alphabet
la gramática	grammar
la ortografía	spelling
la mayúscula	capital letter
la palabra	word
la frase	sentence
el punto	period

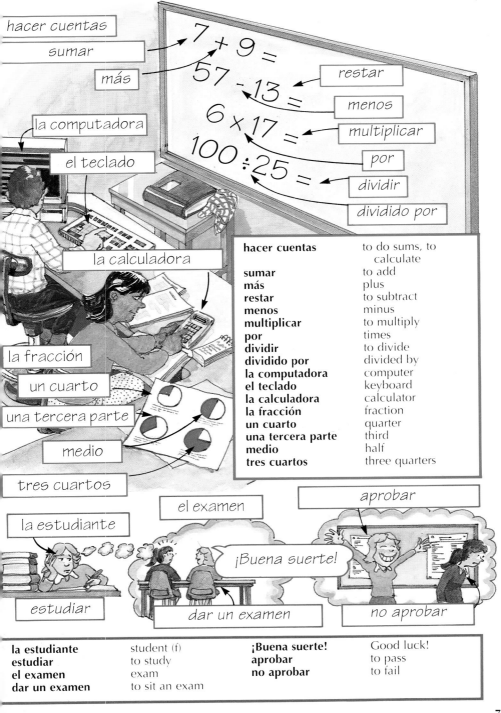

hacer cuentas

sumar

más

$$7 + 9 =$$
$$57 - 13 =$$
$$6 \times 17 =$$
$$100 \div 25 =$$

restar

menos

multiplicar

por

dividir

dividido por

la computadora

el teclado

la calculadora

la fracción

un cuarto

una tercera parte

medio

tres cuartos

hacer cuentas	to do sums, to calculate
sumar	to add
más	plus
restar	to subtract
menos	minus
multiplicar	to multiply
por	times
dividir	to divide
dividido por	divided by
la computadora	computer
el teclado	keyboard
la calculadora	calculator
la fracción	fraction
un cuarto	quarter
una tercera parte	third
medio	half
tres cuartos	three quarters

el examen

aprobar

la estudiante

¡Buena suerte!

estudiar

dar un examen

no aprobar

la estudiante	student (f)	¡Buena suerte!	Good luck!
estudiar	to study	aprobar	to pass
el examen	exam	no aprobar	to fail
dar un examen	to sit an exam		

Shapes and sizes

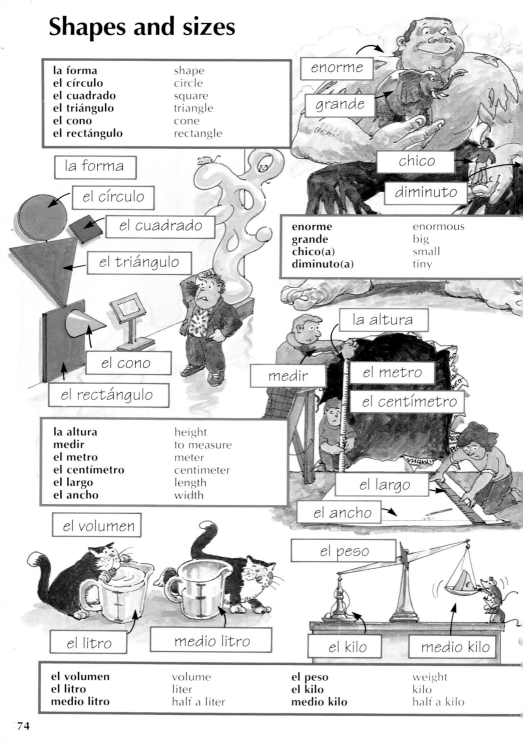

la forma	shape
el círculo	circle
el cuadrado	square
el triángulo	triangle
el cono	cone
el rectángulo	rectangle

enorme

grande

chico

diminuto

enorme	enormous
grande	big
chico(a)	small
diminuto(a)	tiny

la forma

el círculo

el cuadrado

el triángulo

el cono

el rectángulo

la altura

medir

el metro

el centímetro

el largo

el ancho

la altura	height
medir	to measure
el metro	meter
el centímetro	centimeter
el largo	length
el ancho	width

el volumen

el peso

el litro

medio litro

el kilo

medio kilo

el volumen	volume	**el peso**	weight
el litro	liter	**el kilo**	kilo
medio litro	half a liter	**medio kilo**	half a kilo

74

Numbers

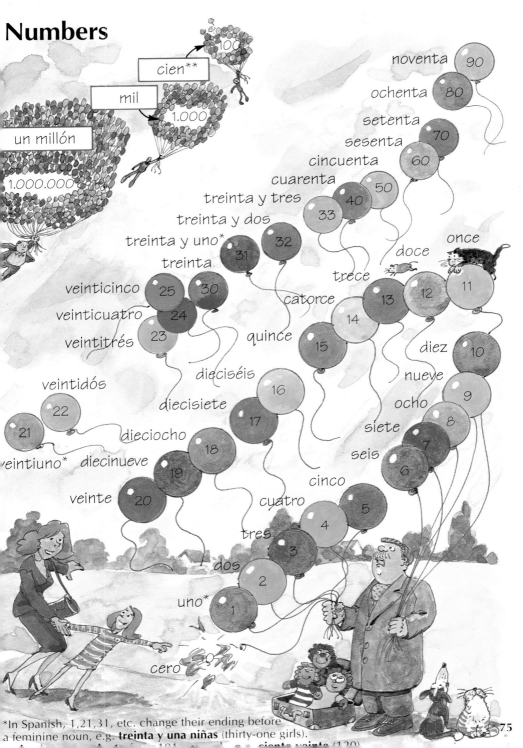

cien** 100

mil 1.000

un millón 1.000.000

noventa 90

ochenta 80

setenta

sesenta 70

cincuenta 60

cuarenta 50

treinta y tres 40

treinta y dos 33

treinta y uno* 32

treinta 31

veinticinco 25 30

veinticuatro 24

veintitrés 23

veintidós 22

veintiuno* 21

veinte 20

diecinueve 19

dieciocho 18

diecisiete 17

dieciséis 16

quince 15

catorce 14

trece 13

doce 12

once 11

diez 10

nueve 9

ocho 8

siete 7

seis 6

cinco 5

cuatro 4

tres 3

dos 2

uno* 1

cero

*In Spanish, 1,21,31, etc. change their ending before
a feminine noun, e.g. **treinta y una niñas** (thirty-one girls).

**cirnto veinte (120)

75

Sports

mantenerse en forma	to keep fit	**la cinta**	headband
entrenarse	to exercise	**las zapatillas**	running shoes
hacer fúting	to jog	**el equipo de deporte**	tracksuit

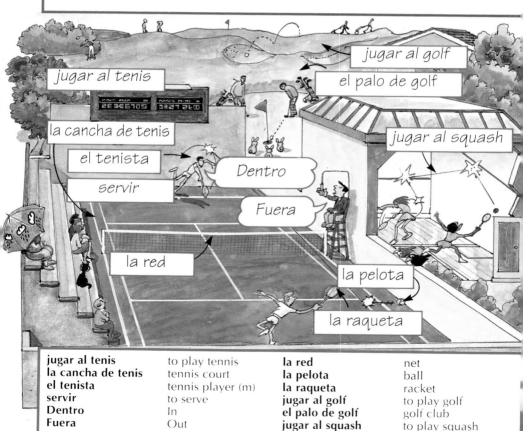

jugar al tenis	to play tennis	**la red**	net
la cancha de tenis	tennis court	**la pelota**	ball
el tenista	tennis player (m)	**la raqueta**	racket
servir	to serve	**jugar al golf**	to play golf
Dentro	In	**el palo de golf**	golf club
Fuera	Out	**jugar al squash**	to play squash

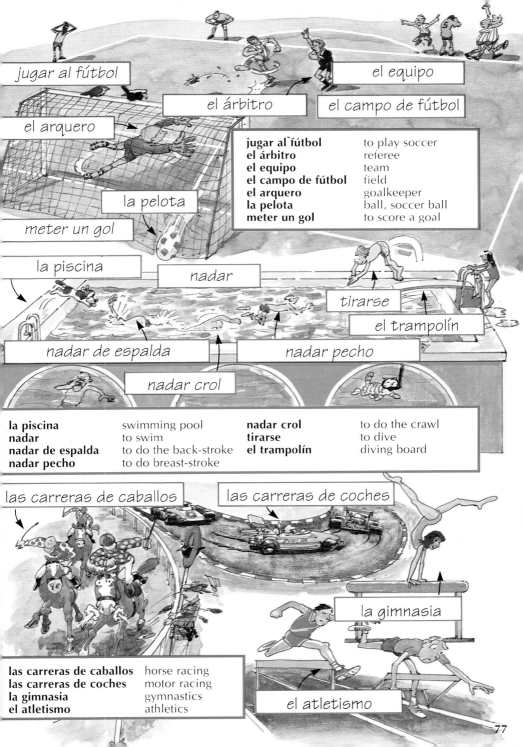

jugar al fútbol

el equipo

el árbitro

el campo de fútbol

el arquero

jugar al fútbol	to play soccer
el árbitro	referee
el equipo	team
el campo de fútbol	field
el arquero	goalkeeper
la pelota	ball, soccer ball
meter un gol	to score a goal

la pelota

meter un gol

la piscina

nadar

tirarse

el trampolín

nadar de espalda

nadar pecho

nadar crol

la piscina	swimming pool		**nadar crol**	to do the crawl
nadar	to swim		**tirarse**	to dive
nadar de espalda	to do the back-stroke		**el trampolín**	diving board
nadar pecho	to do breast-stroke			

las carreras de caballos

las carreras de coches

la gimnasia

el atletismo

las carreras de caballos	horse racing
las carreras de coches	motor racing
la gimnasia	gymnastics
el atletismo	athletics

77

Celebrations

el cumpleaños	birthday
la fiesta	party
el globo	balloon
¡Felicidades!	Congratulations!
invitar	to invite
divertirse	to have fun, to enjoy yourself
el pastel	cake
la vela	candle
la tarjeta	card
el regalo	present
el papel de envolver	wrapping paper

el cumpleaños

la fiesta

el globo

¡Felicidades!

invitar

divertirse

el pastel

la vela

el regalo

el papel de envolver

la tarjeta

el Día de Navidad

Pascua

las Navidades

los Reyes Magos

el árbol de Navidad

Pascua	Easter
las Navidades	Christmas
el Día de Navidad	Christmas Day
los Reyes Magos	the Three Wise Men
el árbol de Navidad	Christmas tree

comprometerse	to get engaged
la boda	wedding
casarse	to get married
el novio	bridegroom
la novia	bride
el invitado	guest (m)
felicitar	to congratulate
el ramo de flores	bouquet
ser feliz	to be happy
el viaje de novios	honeymoon

¡Feliz Navidad!	Merry Christmas!
el villancico	carol
regalar	to give (a present)
recibir	to receive
¡Muchas gracias!	Thank you.
dar las gracias	to thank

Nochevieja	New Year's Eve
el día de Año Nuevo	New Year's Day
celebrar	to celebrate
¡Feliz Año Nuevo!	Happy New Year!

Days and Dates

el calendario

el mes

enero
febrero
marzo
abril
mayo
junio
julio
agosto
setiembre
octubre
noviembre
diciembre

el año

el calendario	calendar
el mes	month
enero	January
febrero	February
marzo	March
abril	April
mayo	May
junio	June
julio	July
agosto	August
setiembre	September
octubre	October
noviembre	November
diciembre	December
el año	year
el día	day
la semana	week
el fin de semana	weekend
lunes (m)	Monday
martes (m)	Tuesday
miércoles (m)	Wednesday
jueves (m)	Thursday
viernes (m)	Friday
sábado (m)	Saturday
domingo (m)	Sunday

lunes

el día

martes
miércoles

la semana

jueves
viernes
sábado
domingo

el fin de semana

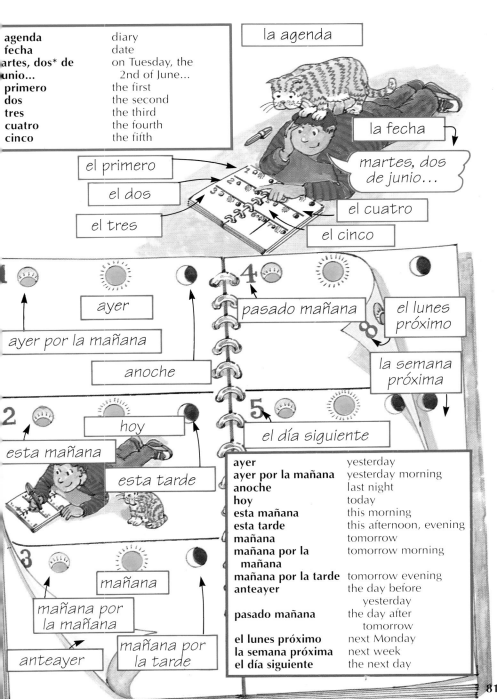

agenda	diary
fecha	date
martes, dos* de junio...	on Tuesday, the 2nd of June...
primero	the first
dos	the second
tres	the third
cuatro	the fourth
cinco	the fifth

la agenda

la fecha

martes, dos de junio...

el primero

el dos

el tres

el cuatro

el cinco

ayer

ayer por la mañana

anoche

pasado mañana

el lunes próximo

la semana próxima

hoy

esta mañana

esta tarde

el día siguiente

ayer	yesterday
ayer por la mañana	yesterday morning
anoche	last night
hoy	today
esta mañana	this morning
esta tarde	this afternoon, evening
mañana	tomorrow
mañana por la mañana	tomorrow morning
mañana por la tarde	tomorrow evening
anteayer	the day before yesterday
pasado mañana	the day after tomorrow
el lunes próximo	next Monday
la semana próxima	next week
el día siguiente	the next day

mañana

mañana por la mañana

anteayer

mañana por la tarde

*You would always write **martes 2 de junio**, but this shows you how to say it.

Time

el amanecer	dawn	**el sol**	sun
la salida del sol	sunrise	**el cielo**	sky
Amanece.	It's getting light.	**Es de día.**	It's light.
la mañana	morning	**el día**	day, daytime

la tarde	afternoon, evening	**las estrellas**	stars
la puesta del sol	sunset	**la luna**	moon
Oscurece.	It's getting dark.	**Es de noche.**	It's dark.
la noche	night		

el minuto

la hora

¿Qué hora es?

el segundo

Es la una.

Son las tres.

mediodía

medianoche

9 : 45 — las diez menos cuarto

10 : 05 — las diez y cinco

10 : 15 — las diez y cuarto

10 : 30 — las diez y media

las ocho de la mañana

las ocho de la tarde

¿Qué hora es?	What time is it?	las diez menos cuarto	a quarter to ten
la hora	hour	las diez y cinco	five past ten
el minuto	minute	las diez y cuarto	a quarter past ten
el segundo	second	las diez y media	half past ten
Es la una.	It's 1 o'clock.	las ocho de la mañana	8 a.m.
Son las tres.	It's 3 o'clock.		
mediodía	midday	las ocho de la tarde	8 p.m.
medianoche	midnight		

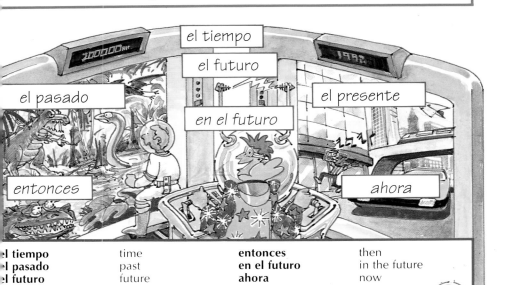

el tiempo

el futuro

el pasado

en el futuro

el presente

entonces

ahora

el tiempo	time	entonces	then
el pasado	past	en el futuro	in the future
el futuro	future	ahora	now
el presente	present		

83

Weather and seasons

la estación	season
la primavera	spring
el verano	summer
el otoño	fall
el invierno	winter

la estación

la primavera

el tiempo

Llueve.

el invierno

la lluvia

la tormenta

la nube

el otoño

el verano

los relámpagos

los truenos

el arco iris

el paraguas

las botas
de goma

estar
calado

el charco

la gota de lluvia

el granizo

la inundación

el tiempo	weather
Llueve.	It's raining.
la lluvia	rain
la tormenta	storm
la nube	cloud
los relámpagos	lightning
los truenos	thunder
el paraguas	umbrella
el arco iris	rainbow
las botas de goma	rubber boots
estar calado(a)	to be soaked to the skin
el charco	puddle
la gota de lluvia	raindrop
el granizo	hail
la inundación	flood

84

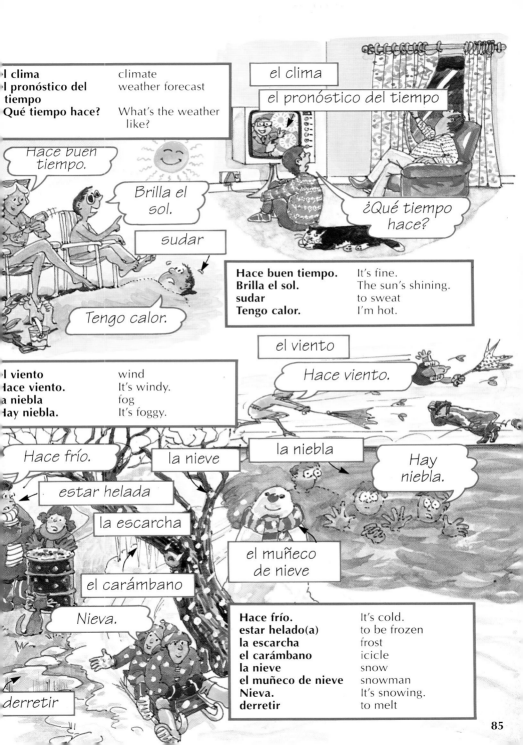

el clima

el pronóstico del tiempo

¿Qué tiempo hace?

el clima	climate
el pronóstico del tiempo	weather forecast
¿Qué tiempo hace?	What's the weather like?

Hace buen tiempo.

Brilla el sol.

sudar

Tengo calor.

Hace buen tiempo.	It's fine.
Brilla el sol.	The sun's shining.
sudar	to sweat
Tengo calor.	I'm hot.

el viento

Hace viento.

el viento	wind
Hace viento.	It's windy.
la niebla	fog
Hay niebla.	It's foggy.

Hace frío.

la nieve

la niebla

Hay niebla.

estar helada

la escarcha

el muñeco de nieve

el carámbano

Nieva.

derretir

Hace frío.	It's cold.
estar helado(a)	to be frozen
la escarcha	frost
el carámbano	icicle
la nieve	snow
el muñeco de nieve	snowman
Nieva.	It's snowing.
derretir	to melt

85

World and universe

el mundo

el polo norte

el norte

el Atlántico

el Pacífico

el oeste

el este

el desierto

el ecuador

la selva

el sur

el polo sur

el mundo	the world	**el norte**	north
el Atlántico	Atlantic Ocean	**el Pacífico**	Pacific Ocean
el oeste	west	**el este**	east
el desierto	desert	**el ecuador**	Equator
la selva	jungle	**el sur**	south
el polo norte	North Pole	**el polo sur**	South Pole

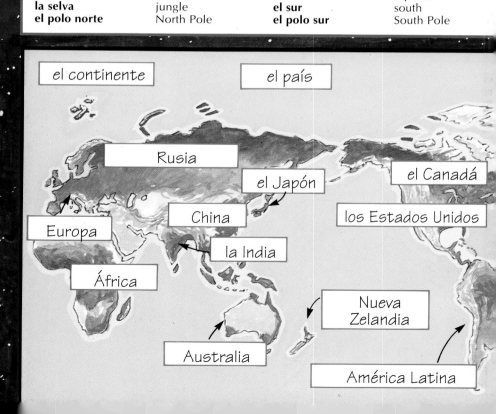

el continente

el país

Rusia

el Japón

el Canadá

China

los Estados Unidos

Europa

la India

África

Nueva
Zelandia

Australia

América Latina

el universo

el espacio

la estrella

el planeta

la nave espacial

la galaxia

el telescopio

el universo	universe
el espacio	space
el planeta	planet
la estrella	star
la nave espacial	spaceship
la galaxia	galaxy
el telescopio	telescope

el continente	continent
el país	country
Rusia	Russia
Europa	Europe
África	Africa
el Japón	Japan
China	China
la India	India
Australia	Australia
Nueva Zelandia	New Zealand
el Canadá	Canada
los Estados Unidos	United States
América Latina	Latin America

Escandinavia	Scandinavia
Gran Bretaña	Great Britain
Holanda	Netherlands
Bélgica	Belgium
Alemania	Germany
Francia	France
Suiza	Switzerland
Italia	Italy
España	Spain
Austria	Austria

Escandinavia

Gran Bretaña

Bélgica / Holanda

Francia

Alemania

Suiza

Austria

Italia

España

Politics

el presidente

el parlamento

la diputada

el primer ministro

el gobierno

el presidente	president (m)
el parlamento	parliament
la diputada	member of parliament (f)
el primer ministro	prime minister (m)
el gobierno	government

el partido

la líder

popular

el miembro

el partido	party
la líder	leader (f)
popular	popular
el miembro	member (m/f)

las elecciones

votar

de izquierda

de centro

de derecha

asociarse

pertenecer a

ganar

perder

las elecciones	election	de centro	center
votar	to vote	de derecha	right wing
ganar	to win	asociarse	to join
perder	to lose	pertenecer a	to belong to
de izquierda	left wing		

los medios de comunicación	media
entrevistar	to interview
importante	important
interesante	interesting
el periódico	newspaper
las noticias	news
los titulares	headlines
el artículo	article
verdadero(a)	true
falso(a)	false

los medios de comunicación

entrevistar

importante

interesante

el periódico

las noticias

los titulares

el artículo

verdadero

falso

@*&!!# ?*&!!

el salario

los impuestos

&#?!

la política

la sociedad

el sindicato

el desempleo

democrática

la política	politics	los impuestos	taxes
la sociedad	society	el sindicato	labor union
democrático(a)	democratic	el desempleo	unemployment
el salario	salary, wages		

Describing things

ruidoso

callado

obediente

travieso

iguales

ruidoso(a)	noisy
callado(a)	quiet
obediente	obedient
travieso(a)	naughty
igual	same
diferente	different

diferentes

juntos

solo

ocupado

útil

asustado

ocupado(a)	busy
útil	useful
juntos(as)	together
solo(a)	alone
asustado(a)	frightened
valiente	brave

valiente

descuidado

cuidadoso

enojada

animado

contenta con

aburrido

descuidado(a)	careless
cuidadoso(a)	careful
enojado(a)	angry
contento(a) con	pleased with
animado(a)	lively
aburrido(a)	bored, boring

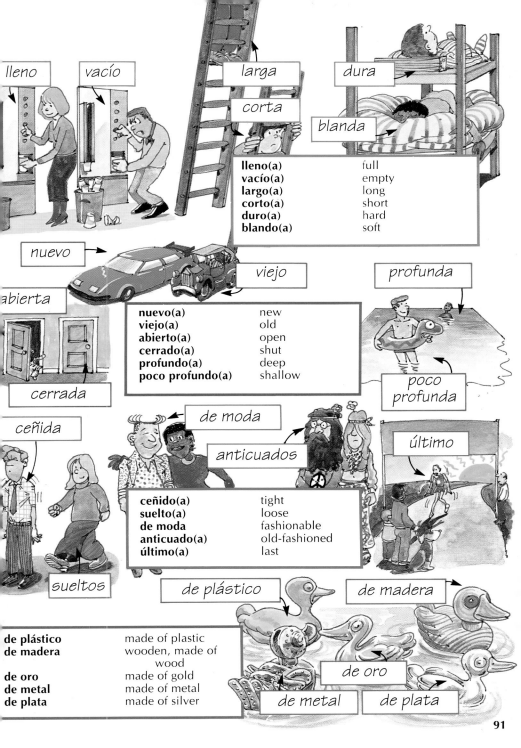

lleno

vacío

larga

dura

corta

blanda

lleno(a)	full
vacío(a)	empty
largo(a)	long
corto(a)	short
duro(a)	hard
blando(a)	soft

nuevo

viejo

profunda

abierta

nuevo(a)	new
viejo(a)	old
abierto(a)	open
cerrado(a)	shut
profundo(a)	deep
poco profundo(a)	shallow

cerrada

poco profunda

ceñida

de moda

último

anticuados

ceñido(a)	tight
suelto(a)	loose
de moda	fashionable
anticuado(a)	old-fashioned
último(a)	last

sueltos

de plástico

de madera

de plástico	made of plastic
de madera	wooden, made of wood
de oro	made of gold
de metal	made of metal
de plata	made of silver

de oro

de metal

de plata

91

Colors

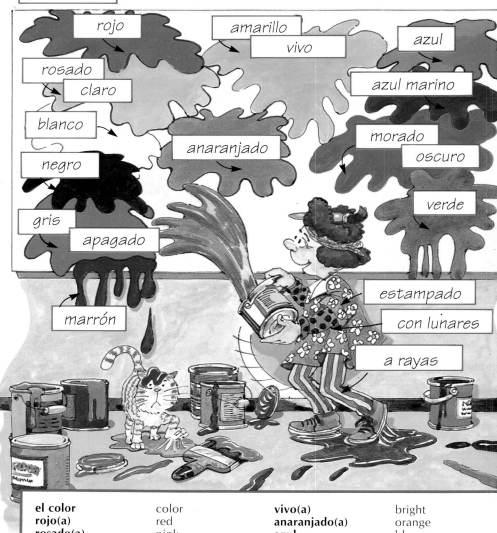

el color

rojo

amarillo

vivo

azul

rosado

claro

azul marino

blanco

anaranjado

morado

oscuro

negro

gris

verde

apagado

estampado

con lunares

marrón

a rayas

el color	color	**vivo(a)**	bright
rojo(a)	red	**anaranjado(a)**	orange
rosado(a)	pink	**azul**	blue
claro(a)	pale	**azul marino**	navy blue
blanco(a)	white	**morado(a)**	purple
negro(a)	black	**oscuro(a)**	dark
gris	gray	**verde**	green
apagado(a)	dull	**estampado(a)**	printed
marrón	brown	**con lunares**	spotted
amarillo(a)	yellow	**a rayas**	striped

In, on, under...

en

sobre

debajo de

dentro

por encima de

fuera

al lado de

cerca de

delante de

etrás de

entre

lejos de

por

hacia

contra

entre

con

de

abajo

arriba

frente a

sin

en	in	**detrás de**	behind
sobre	on	**contra**	against
debajo de	under	**por**	through
por encima de	over	**entre**	among
dentro	into	**hacia**	to, toward
fuera	out of	**de**	from
al lado de	beside	**arriba**	up
entre	between	**abajo**	down
cerca de	near	**frente a**	opposite
lejos de	far away from	**con**	with
delante de	in front of	**sin**	without

Action words

cuchichear

gritar

buscar

esperar

apoyarse en

sostener

cuchichear	to whisper
gritar	to shout
buscar	to look for
esperar	to wait for
apoyarse en	to lean on
sostener	to hold

llevar

recoger

dejar caer

dejar

| llevar | to carry | | recoger | to pick up |
| dejar caer | to drop | | dejar | to leave |

tocar

cerrar

abrir

echar

llenar

sacudir

vaciar

tocar	to touch
abrir	to open
cerrar	to close
echar	to pour, throw
llenar	to fill
sacudir	to shake
vaciar	to empty

rasgar	to tear
zurcir	to mend
tirar	to throw
agarrar	to catch
volcar	to knock over
romper	to break

tirar	to pull	escapar	to run away
empujar	to push	seguir	to follow
robar	to steal	esconderse	to hide
resbalar	to slip		

Grammar hints

In order to speak Spanish well, you need to learn a little about the grammar, that is, how you put words together and make sentences. On the next few pages there are some hints on Spanish grammar. Don't worry if you cannot remember them all at first. Try to learn a little grammar at a time and then practise using it.

Nouns

In Spanish all nouns are either masculine or feminine. The word you use for "the" is **el** before a masculine noun and **la** before a feminine noun*:

el vaso	glass
la mesa	table

Most nouns ending in **-o** are masculine and those ending in **-a** are feminine. Nouns ending in **-e** may be masculine or feminine:

la calle	street
el parque	park

Nouns which describe what people are or what they do usually have a masculine and a feminine form:

el amigo	friend (m)
la amiga	friend (f)
el conductor	driver (m)
la conductora	driver (f)
el bailarín	dancer (m)
la bailarina	dancer (f)

Sometimes this type of noun uses the same form for both masculine and feminine:

el estudiante	student (m)
la estudiante	student (f)
el turista	tourist (m)
la turista	tourist (f)
el dentista	dentist (m)
la dentista	dentist (f)

When these nouns appear in the illustrated section, only the form which matches with the picture is given, but both the masculine and the feminine are given in the word list at the back of the book.

Plurals

When you are talking about more than one thing, the word for "the" is **los** for masculine nouns and **las** for feminine nouns:

los vasos
las mesas

To make nouns plural, you usually add **s** to those ending in a vowel, and **es** to those ending in a consonant:

la calle	street
las calles	streets
la ciudad	city
las ciudades	cities

*Feminine nouns that begin with a stressed **a** use **el** not **la** for "the", e.g. **el águila** the eagle, **el agua** the water.

a, an, some

The word for "a" is **un** before a masculine noun and **una** before a feminine noun:

un vaso
una mesa

The word for some is **unos** before a masculine plural noun and **unas** before a feminine plural noun:

unos vasos
unas mesas

this, that

"This" is **este** before a masculine noun and **esta** before a feminine noun. The plural, "these", is **estos** before a masculine noun and **estas** before a feminine noun:

este vaso   **estos vasos**
esta mesa   **estas mesas**

"That" is **ese** before a masculine noun and **esa** before a feminine noun. The plural, "those", is **esos** before a masculine noun and **esas** before a feminine noun:

ese vaso   **esos vasos**
esa mesa   **esas mesas**

In Spanish there is another word for "that", **aquel**. **Aquel** is used when you are talking about something that is far away from both you and the person you are speaking to:

aquel vaso   **aquellos vasos**
aquella mesa   **aquellas mesas**

my, your

"My", "your", "his", "her", "our" and "their" are called possessive adjectives. In Spanish they change according to whether the noun which follows is singular or plural:

s	pl
my	
(m) mi amigo	**mis amigos**
my friend	my friends
(f) mi hermana	**mis hermanas**
my sister	my sisters
your (informal*, s)	
tu amigo	**tus amigos**
tu hermana	**tus hermanas**
his/her/its/your (formal*, s)	
su amigo	**sus amigos**
su hermana	**sus hermanas**
our	
nuestro amigo	**nuestros amigos**
nuestra hermana	**nuestras hermanas**
your (pl); their	
su amigo	**sus amigos**
su hermana	**sus hermanas**

*See pronouns on page 98.

Adjectives

Adjectives are describing words. In Spanish, adjectives usually follow the noun they are describing. They also change their endings depending on whether they are describing a masculine or a feminine noun and whether it is singular or plural. Most adjectives end in **-o** in the masculine and this **-o** changes to **-a** in the feminine:

un vecino simpático	a pleasant neighbour
una película aburrida	a boring film

Adjectives ending in "e" or a consonant don't change in the feminine:

el vaso grande	the big glass
la mesa grande	the big table
el vestido gris	the grey dress
la corbata gris	the grey tie

The following adjectives showing nationality end in a consonant but do take an "a" in the feminine:

m	f	
alemán	**alemana**	German
español	**española**	Spanish
francés	**francesa**	French
inglés	**inglesa**	English
irlandés	**irlandesa**	Irish
holandés	**holandesa**	Dutch
portugués	**portuguesa**	Portuguese

To make adjectives plural, you add **s** if it ends in a vowel and **es** if it ends in a consonant:

los vecinos simpáticos
las corbatas grises

Comparing adjectives

To compare things, you put **tan... como** (as... as), **más... que** (more... than) and **el, la, los** or **las más** (the most) with an adjective. The adjective agrees in the usual way:

Ella es tan alta como su hermano.
She is as tall as her brother.
Ella es más delgada que yo.
She is slimmer than I am.
Soy el más guapo.
I am the best looking.

Just as in English, some common adjectives do not add **más** (more) or **el más**, but change completely:

bueno	good
mejor	better
el mejor	the best
malo	bad
peor	worse
el peor	the worst

Pronouns

"I", "you", "he", "she" and so on are called personal pronouns. In Spanish there are several words for "you". In the singular, **tú** is informal and is most commonly used. **Usted** is formal and is used when you are talking to people in authority, strangers or older people.

Ustedes can be formal or informal in Latin America. **Usted** and **ustedes** are often written **Ud.** and **Uds.**, or **Vd.** and **Vds.**.

yo	I
tú	you (informal, s)
él	he
ella	she
Usted (Vd.)	you (formal, s)
nosotros/as	we (m/f)
Ustedes (Vds.)	you (pl)
ellos	they (m)
ellas	they (f)

Verbs

Spanish verbs (action words) change their endings according to who is doing the action. The pronoun, "I", "you" and so on is often left out because the ending of the verb tells you who is doing the action.
Most verbs follow regular patterns of endings. There are three patterns according to whether the verb's infinitve (e.g. in English: "to buy"; "to eat") ends in **-ar**, **-er** or **-ir**. These are the endings for the present tense:

comprar	to buy
compro	I buy
compras	you (informal, s) buy
compra	he, she buys;
	you (formal, s) buy
compramos	we buy
compran	you (pl) buy
compran	they buy

comer to eat	**subir** to climb
como	**subo**
comes	**subes**
come	**sube**
comemos	**subimos**
comen	**suben**
comen	**suben**

Some of the most common verbs do not follow these patterns in the present tense. They are known as irregular verbs and you need to learn them separately.

Two common irregular verbs are **ser** and **estar**. These both mean "to be", but are used in different ways. You use **ser** to describe things or people, and to present yourself or others: e.g. "My room is green"; "I am Spanish"; "my father is a dentist"; "Lucy is a vegetarian". **Estar** is used to describe things that can change: e.g. "I am tired"; "The room is messy"; "The drink is cold". **Estar** is also used to say where things are: e.g. "The cinema is over there"; "I am here".

Here are the present tenses of **ser** and **estar**:

ser	**estar**
soy	**estoy**
eres	**estás**
es	**está**
somos	**estamos**
son	**están**
son	**están**

You can find other irregular verbs on page 106.

Estar is also used to make the present progressive. This is a tense that the Spanish use to stress something that is being done now, e.g. "I am walking", "I am reading this book". To make this tense, you use the present tense of **estar** (as shown on page 99) and the "ing" form of the verb you want to use, which is made by adding **-ando** to the stem of **-ar** verbs and **-iendo** to the stem of **-ir** and **-er** verbs*. (The stem is the first part of the verb, without the **-ar**, **-er** or **-ir** ending). For example:

estoy comprando I am buying
estamos comiendo we are eating
está subiendo la   he is going up
  escalera   the stairs

The future tense is used for things you are going to do. It is the same for the three verb types, and it is made by adding these endings to the infinitive:

comprar é
comprar ás
comprar á
comprar emos
comprar án
comprar án

To talk about things in the past, the Spanish usually use the preterite (for things that happened once only or at a specific time, e.g. "One day a dog ran out and bit me"; "Yesterday I went to the cinema") or the imperfect tense (for things that were happening over a period of time, for describing people or objects or for describing things you used to do,

e.g. "When I was walking along the road..."; "He had a beard and was wearing a hat"; "When we were five we used to play together").

To form the imperfect you take the stem of the verb (ie the infinitive minus the **-ar**, **-ir** or **-er** ending) and add the following endings:

For **-ar** verbs add **-aba**, **-abas**, **-aba**, **-ábamos**, **-aban**, **-aban**, e.g.:

compraba	I was buying; I used to buy
comprabas	you (informal, s) were buying; you used to buy
compraba	he/she was buying, you (formal, s) were buying; he/she/you used to buy
comprábamos	we were buying; we used to buy
compraban	you (pl) were buying; you used to buy
compraban	they were buying; they used to buy

For **-ir** and **-er** verbs add **-ía**, **-ías**, **-ía**, **-íamos**, **-ían**, **-ían**, e.g.:

subía	I was climbing; I used to climb
subías	you (informal, s) were climbing; you used to climb
subía	he/she was climbing, you (formal, s) were climbing; he/she/you used to climb
subíamos	we were climbing; we used to climb

*When the stem of an **ir** or **er** verb ends in a vowel, **iendo** changes to **yendo**, e.g. **leer**, to read, becomes **leyendo**, reading.

| subían | you (pl) were climbing; you used to climb |
| subían | they were climbing; they used to climb |

To form the preterite you take the stem of the verb and add the following endings:

For **-ar** verbs add **-é**, **-aste**, **-ó**, **-amos**, **-aron**, **-aron**, e.g.:

compré	I bought
compraste	you (informal, s) bought
compró	he/she bought, you (formal, s) bought
compramos	we bought
compraron	you (pl) bought
compraron	they bought

For **-ir** and **-er** verbs add **-í**, **-iste**, **-ió**, **-imos**, **-ieron**, **-ieron**, e.g.:

subí	I climbed
subiste	you (informal, s) climbed
subió	he/she climbed, you (formal, s) climbed
subimos	we climbed
subieron	you (pl) climbed
subieron	they climbed

The present perfect is another past tense used to talk about things you have done, for example "we have bought", "he has climbed". You make it using the present tense of a special verb **haber**, which is **he**, **has**, **ha**, **hemos**, **han**, **han**, and the past participle, which you make using the stem of the verb plus **-ado** for **-ar** verbs and **-ido** for **-er** and **-ir** verbs.

For example:

he comprado	I have bought
has comprado	you (informal, s) have bought
ha comprado	he/she has bought, you (formal, s) have bought
hemos comprado	we have bought
han comprado	you (pl) have bought
han comprado	they have bought

he subido	I have climbed
has subido	you (informal, s) have climbed
ha subido	he/she has climbed, you (formal, s) have climbed
hemos subido	we have climbed
han subido	you (pl) have climbed
han subido	they have climbed

he comido	I have eaten
has comido	you (informal, pl) have eaten
ha comido	he/she has eaten, you (formal, s) have eaten
hemos comido	we have eaten
han comido	you (pl) have eaten
han comido	they have eaten

Reflexive verbs

Verbs which have **se** at the end of the infinitive are called reflexive verbs. These verbs usually involve doing something to yourself (e.g. in English: "to wash oneself"), but you will find that far more verbs can be reflexive in Spanish than in English.

lavarse	to wash oneself
peinarse	to comb one's hair
afeitarse	to shave
levantarse	to get up
dormirse	to fall asleep

Se means "self" and changes according to who is doing the action (as it does in English):

yo me lavo	I wash myself
tú te lavas	you (informal, s) wash yourself
él, ella se lava	he/she washes him/herself
Usted se lava	you (formal, s) wash yourself
nosotros nos lavamos	we wash ourselves
Ustedes se lavan	you (pl) wash yourselves
ellos, ellas se lavan	they (m/f) wash themselves

Negatives

To make a negative in Spanish, you put **no** before the whole verb. If the verb is reflexive, **no** goes before the reflexive pronoun (**me**, **te**, **se**, etc.):

No hablamos inglés.
We do not speak English.
No ha pagado.
He has not paid.
No se lava las manos.
She doesn't wash her hands.
No se bañaron ayer.
They didn't swim yesterday.

Object pronouns

An object pronoun is a word which is used to replace a noun that is the object of a verb:

Yo prefiero el queso.
I prefer cheese.
Yo lo prefiero.
I prefer it.

These are the object pronouns in Spanish:

me	me
te	you (informal, s)
lo	him, it
la	her, it
lo, **la**	you (formal, s m/f)
nos	us (m/f)
los, **las**	you (pl m/f)
los	them (m)
las	them (f)

In Spanish you put the object pronoun just before the verb. If the verb is reflexive, the object pronoun goes after the reflexive pronoun.

Lo estoy buscando.
I am looking for it.
No lo encuentro.
I can't find it.
Lo he comprado.
I have bought it.
Me lavo las manos.
I am washing my hands.
Me las lavo.
I am washing them.

Questions

In Spanish you can make a question simply by raising your voice at the end of a sentence:

¿Quieres otro helado?
Do you want another ice cream?/
Would you like another ice cream?
¿No has empezado aún?
Haven't you started yet?
¿Lo has perdido?
Have you lost it?

When a question is written down, as well as ending with a question mark, it starts with an upside down question mark. (Note that Spanish exclamation marks are used in the same way.)

Below are some common question words. When you use these, you put the subject after the whole verb (but remember, if the subject is "I", "you", etc, it is usually left out):

¿Cómo...?
How...?
¿Cómo hiciste eso?
How did you do that?
¿Cuándo...?
When...?
¿Cuándo es la fiesta?
When is the party?
¿Cuánto...?
How much...?
¿Cuánto es esto?
How much is this?
¿Dónde...?
Where...?
¿Dónde estuviste ayer?
Where were you yesterday?
¿Qué...?
What...?
¿Qué está haciendo Pablo?
What is Pablo doing?
¿Quién...?
Who...?
¿Quién llegó primero?
Who arrived first?
¿Por qué...?
Why...?
¿Por qué no nos encontramos luego?
Why don't we meet later?

Stem-changing verbs

There is a group of verbs in Spanish in which the last vowel in the stem changes in the present tense (except in the "we" form). Verbs of this sort are called stem-changing verbs and you need to learn to recognize and use them. In verbs that have **e** as the last vowel in the stem, the **e** changes to **ie**, or in a few cases to **i**. In verbs that have **o** as the last vowel in their stem, the **o** changes to **ue**.

Here are the present tenses of **cerrar** which has an **e** that changes to **ie**, **medir** with an **e** that changes to **i**, and **encontrar** with an **o** that changes to **ue**.

cerrar (ie)   to shut

cierro
cierras
cierra
cerramos
cierran
cierran

medir (i)   to measure

mido
mides
mide
medimos
miden
miden

encontrar (ue)   to find

encuentro
encuentras
encuentra
encontramos
encuentran
encuentran

The verbs in the list below have an **e** that changes to **ie** as in **cerrar**:

deshelar	to thaw
despertarse	to wake up
divertirse	to enjoy oneself
empezar	to begin
encender	to turn on, to light
fregar	to rub, to scrub
helar	to freeze
negarse	to refuse
nevar	to snow
pensar	to think
perder	to lose
preferir	to prefer
querer	to want, o love (see page 106)
sentarse	to sit down
sentirse	to feel
temblar	to tremble, to shake
verter	to pour, to spill

* In the first person singular of **perseguir** and **seguir** there is no **u** after the **g**: **yo persigo, yo sigo.**

The verbs in this list have an **e** that changes to **i**, as in **medir**:

despedirse	to say goodbye
pedir	to ask for
reírse	to laugh
repetir	to repeat
perseguir*	to chase
seguir*	to follow
sonreír	to smile
vestirse	to dress

The verbs in this list have an **o** that changes to **ue**, as in **encontrar**:

acostarse	to go to bed
colgar	to hang
contar	to tell a story, to count
costar	to cost
devolver	to give back
envolver	to wrap up
jugar	to play
(**u** becomes **ue**)	
llover	to rain
morder	to bite
morir	to die
mover	to move
oler	to smell
(**o** becomes **hue**)	
probar	to try, to prove
recordar	to remember, to remind
soñar	to dream
torcer*	to twist
volar	to fly
volcar	to knock over, to overturn
volver	to return

Irregular verbs

Here are the present tenses of some common irregular verbs, together with the **yo** form of the future, preterite, imperfect and perfect tenses where they are irregular. Try to learn these verbs as you will probably need to use them quite frequently when you are speaking Spanish.

caer   to fall

caigo
caes
cae
caemos
caen
caen

preterite: in the third person only the **i** changes to **y**: **cayó**, **cayeron**, he fell, they fell.

dar   to give

doy
das
da
damos
dan
dan

preterite: **di**

---

* In the first person singular of **torcer** the middle **c** changes to a **z**: **yo tuerzo**.

decir	to say	**ir**	to go

digo		**voy**	
dices		**vas**	
dice		**va**	
decimos		**vamos**	
dicen		**van**	
dicen		**van**	

future: **diré**
preterite: **dije**
perfect: **he dicho**

preterite: **fui**
imperfect: **iba**

oír to hear

estar to be

oigo

estoy   **oyes**
estás   **oye**
está   **oímos**
estamos   **oyen**
están   **oyen**
están

preterite: in the third person only
the **i** changes to **y** : **oyó**, **oyeron**

preterite: **estuve**

hacer to do, to make   **poder** to be able to

hago   **puedo**
haces   **puedes**
hace   **puede**
hacemos   **podemos**
hacen   **pueden**
hacen   **pueden**

future: **haré**   future: **podré**
preterite: **hice**   preterite: **pude**
perfect: **he hecho**

poner to put

pongo
pones
pone
ponemos
ponen
ponen

future: **pondré**
perfect: **he puesto**

querer to want, to love

quiero
quieres
quiere
queremos
quieren
quieren

future: **querré**
preterite: **quise**

saber to know

sé
sabes
sabe
sabemos
saben
saben

future: **sabré**
preterite: **supe**

salir to go out

salgo
sales
sale
salimos
salen
salen

future: **saldré**

ser to be

soy
eres
es
somos
son
son

preterite: **fui**
imperfect: **era**

tener to have, to hold

tengo
tienes
tiene
tenemos
tienen
tienen

future: **tendré**
preterite: **tuve**

traer	to bring
traigo	
traes	
trae	
traemos	
traen	
traen	

preterite: **traje**

venir	to come
vengo	
vienes	
viene	
venimos	
vienen	
vienen	

future: **vendré**
preterite: **vine**

ver	to see
veo	
ves	
ve	
vemos	
ven	
ven	

perfect: **he visto**

A few verbs are only irregular in the present perfect:

abrir	to open
he abierto	I have opened

escribir	to write
he escrito	I have written

volver	to come back
he vuelto	I have come back

A few verbs are irregular in the present progressive (I am doing something). You add the following participles to the present form of **estar**:

decir	to say
diciendo	saying

pedir	to ask
pidiendo	asking

sentir	to feel
sintiendo	feeling

venir	to come
viniendo	coming

English-Spanish word list

Here you will find all the Spanish words, phrases and expressions from the illustrated section of this book listed in English alphabetical order. Wherever useful, phrases and expressions are cross-referenced, and the words they are made up from are included in the list.

Following each Spanish term, you will find its pronunciation in italics. To pronounce Spanish properly, you need to listen a Spanish-language person speaking. This pronunciation guide will give you an idea as to how to pronounce new words and act as a reminder to words you have heard spoken.

Remember that:
- the Spanish **ñ** is like the *ni* sound in *onion*
- **v** is like an English *b*
- **ll** is said like *y* in *yes* but with a hint of an *l* before it
- **g** (when it precedes an **i** or an **e**) and **j** sound like *ch* in the Scottish *loch* (a guttural *h*)
- **d** (when it is on the end of a word) is very soft, between a *d* and a *t* sound
- **z** is like a soft *s* in English
- **h** is not pronounced
- **r** is always pronounced, including at the end of a word.

When using the pronunciation hints in italics, read them as if they were English "words", but bear in mind the following points:

- it is important in Spanish to stress the correct part of the word: the syllable you should stress is shown in CAPITAL letters
- *a* represents the *a* sound in *happen*
- *e* is like the *e* in *felt*
- *ee* like *ee* in *keen*
- *g* is hard, like the *g* in *get*
- *o* is like the *o* in *holiday*
- *oo* like *oo* in *boot*
- *ch* like *ch* in *loch*
- *ly* like the *ly* sound in *Delia*
- *rrr* represents the Spanish rolled *r*. To say it, make a trilling sound with the tip of your tongue placed behind your top teeth.

A

academic year	**el curso**	*el KOORsso*
actor	**el actor**	*el akTOR*
actress	**la actriz**	*la akTREESS*
to add	**sumar**	*ssooMAR*
address	**la dirección**	*la deerekSSYONN*
adhesive bandage	**la curita**	*la kooREEta*
advertisement	**el anuncio**	*el aNOONssyo*
aeroplane	**el avión**	*el aBYONN*
Africa	**África**	*Afreeka*
afternoon, evening	**la tarde**	*la TARde*
against	**contra**	*KONtra*
age	**la edad**	*la eDAD*
I agree	**De acuerdo**	*de aKWERdo*
airmail	**por avión**	*por aBYONN*
airport	**el aeropuerto**	*el aeroPWERto*
aisle	**la nave**	*la NAbe*
alarm clock	**el despertador**	*el despertaDOR*
alone	**solo(a)**	*SSOlo(a)*
alphabet	**el alfabeto**	*el alfaBEto*
ambulance	**la ambulancia**	*la ambooLANssya*
among	**entre**	*ENtre*
anchor	**el ancla (f)**	*el ANkla*
and	**y**	*ee*
angry	**enojado(a)**	*enoCHAdo(a)*
animal	**el animal**	*el aneeMAL*
ankle	**el tobillo**	*el toBEElyo*
to answer	**contestar**	*kontessTAR*
to answer the telephone	**atender el teléfono**	*atenDER el teLEfono*
apartment	**el apartamento**	*el apartaMENto*
apartment building	**el edificio**	*el edeeFEEssyo*
appetizer	**la entrada**	*la enTRAda*
apple	**la manzana**	*la manSSAna*
apple tree	**el manzano**	*el manSSAno*
apricot	**el chabacano**	*el tshabaKAno*
	el damasco	*el daMASSko*
	el albaricoque	*el albareeKOke*
April	**abril**	*aBREEL*
architect (m)	**el arquitecto**	*el arkeeTEKto*
architect (f)	**la arquitecta**	*la arkeeTEKta*
area code	**el código regional**	*el KOdeego rechyoNAL*
arm	**el brazo**	*el BRAsso*
armchair	**el sillón**	*el sseeLYONN*
Arrivals	**llegadas (f. pl)**	*lyeGAdass*
art gallery	**la galería de arte**	*la galeREEya de ARte*
article (in newspaper)	**el artículo**	*el arTEEkoolo*
to ask, to ask a question	**preguntar**	*pregunTAR*
to ask the way	**preguntar el camino**	*pregunTAR el kaMEEno*
athletics	**el atletismo**	*el atleTEESmo*
Atlantic Ocean	**el Atlántico**	*el atLANteeko*
attic	**el desván**	*el desBAN*
audience	**el público**	*el POObleeko*
August	**agosto**	*aGOSSto*
aunt	**la tía**	*la TEEya*
Australia	**Australia**	*aoossTRALya*
Austria	**Austria**	*AOOsstrya*

B

English	Spanish	Pronunciation
baby	el bebé	el beBE
back	la espalda	la essPALda
backpack	la mochila	la moTSHEEla
backward	hacia atrás	Assya aTRASS
backyard	el jardín	el charDEEN
baggage room	la consigna	la konSSEEGna
bait	el cebo	el SSEbo
bakery	la panadería	la panadeREEya
balcony	el balcón	el balKONN
with balcony	con balcón	kon balKONN
bald	calvo	KALbo(a)
to be bald	ser calvo	sser KALbo
ball	la pelota	la peLOta
ball point pen	el bolígrafo	el boLEEgrafo
ballet	el ballet	el baLE
ballet dancer (m)	el bailarín	el baeelaREEN
ballet dancer (f)	la bailarina	la baeelaREEna
balloon	el globo	el GLObo
banana	el plátano	el PLAtano
bandage	la venda	la BENda
bangs	el flequillo	el fleKEElyo
bank (river)	la orilla	la OREElya
bank	el banco	el BANko
bank manager	el gerente del banco	el cheRENte del BANko
banknote	el billete	el beeLYEte
barefoot	descalzo	dessKALsso
a bargain	una ganga (f)	OOna GANga
to bark	ladrar	laDRAR
barn	el granero	el graNEro
barrier	la barrera	la baRRREra
basement	el sótano	el SSOtano
basket (large)	el cesto	el SSESSto
basket, shopping basket	la cesta	la SSESSta
to bathe	lavarse	laBARsse
bathmat	la alfombrita de baño	la alfombREEta de BAnyo
bathrobe	la bata de baño	la BAta de BAnyo
bathroom	el baño	el BANyo
	el cuarto de baño	el KWARto de BANyo
bathtub	la bañera	la baNYEra
to be	ser	sser
	estar	essTAR
to be born	nacer	naSSER
to be fond of	tenerle cariño a	teNERle kaREENyo a
to be frozen	estar helado(a)	essTAR eLAdo(a)
to be happy	ser feliz	sser feLEESS
to be hungry	tener hambre	teNER AMbre
to be late	llegar tarde	lyeGAR TARde
	estar demorado	essTAR demoRAdo
to be lying down	estar acostado(a)	essTAR acosTAdo(a)
to be on time	llegar a la hora	lyeGAR a la Ora
	llegar a tiempo	lyeGAR a TYEMpo
to be seasick	marearse	mareARsse
to be sick	vomitar	bomeeTAR
to be standing	estar de pie	essTAR de pyE
to be thirsty	tener sed	teNER sed
to be tired	estar cansado(a)	essTAR kanSSAdo(a)
beach	la playa	la PLAya
on the beach	en la playa	en la PLAya
beach umbrella	la sombrilla	la ssomBREElya
beak	el pico	el PEEko
green beans	las habichuelas	lass abeeCHOOElass
kidney beans	los frijoles	loss freeCHOless
bed	la cama	la KAma
to go to bed	acostarse	akossTARsse
bedroom	el dormitorio	el dormeeTORyo
bedside table	la mesita de noche	la meSSEEta de NOtshe
bedspread	la colcha	la KOLtsha
bedtime	la hora de acostarse	la Ora de akossTARsse
bee	la abeja	la aBEcha
beer	la cerveza	la sserBEssa
beginning of course	el principio de curso	el preenSSEEpyo de KOORsso
behind	detrás de	deTRASS de
Belgium	Bélgica	BELcheeka
bell	la campana	la kamPAna
to belong to	pertenecer a	perteneSSER a
belt	el cinturón	el sseentooRONN
safety belt, seatbelt	el cinturón de seguridad	el sseentooRONN de ssegooreeDAD
bench	el banco	el BANko
beside	al lado de	al LAdo de
better	mejor	meCHOR
to feel better	sentirse mejor	ssenTEERsse meCHOR
between	entre	ENtre
Beware of the dog	¡Cuidado con el perro!	kooeeDAdo con el PErrro
bicycle	la bicicleta	la beesseKLEta
big	grande	GRANde
bill (money)	el billete	el beeLYEte
billfold	la billetera	la beelyeTEra
biology	la biología	la beeoloCHEEya
bird	el pájaro	el PAcharo
birth	el nacimiento	el naceeMYENto
birthday	el cumpleaños	el koompleANyoss
birthday card	la tarjeta	la tarCHEta
bitter	agrio(a)	Agryo(a)
black	negro(a)	NEgro(a)
blackbird	el mirlo	el MEERlo
blackboard	la pizarra	la peeSSArrra
blond	rubio(a)	RRROObyo(a)
blond hair	el pelo rubio	el PElo RRROObyo
blouse	la blusa	la BLOOssa
blue	azul	aSSOOL
navy blue	azul marino	aSSOOL maREEno
to board the plane	abordar el avión	aborDAR el aBYONN
board games	los juegos de mesa	loss CHWEgoss de MEssa
boarding house	la pensión	la penSSYONN
body	el cuerpo	el KWERpo
bonnet	el capó	el kapO
book	el libro	el LEEbro
book bag	la cartera	la karTEra
picture book	el libro ilustrado	el LEEbro eelooSTRAdo
booked up, fully booked	completo	komPLEto
bookstore	la librería	la leebreREEya
bookstore and stationer's	la librería y papelería	la leebreREEya ee papeleREEya
boots	las botas	lass BOtass
rubber boots	las botas de goma	lass BOtass de GOma
bored, boring	aburrido(a)	abooRRREEdo(a)
to be born	nacer	naSSER

English	Spanish	Pronunciation
boss (m)	el jefe	el CHEfe
boss (f)	la jefa	la CHEfa
bottle	la botella	la boTElya
bouquet	el ramo de flores	el RRRAmo de FLOress
boutique	la boutique	la booTEEK
bowl	el tazón	el taSSON
box office	la taquilla	la taKEElya
boy	el niño	el NEENyo
bra	el sujetador	el soochetaDOR
bracelet	la pulsera	la poolSSEra
braids	trenzas	TRENssass
branch	la rama	la RRRAma
brave	valiente	baLYENte
Bravo!	¡Bravo!	BRAbo
bread	el pan	el pan
to break	romper	rrromPER
to break your leg	romperse la pierna	rrromPERsse la PYERna
breakdown (vehicle)	la avería	la abeREEya
to have a breakdown	tener una avería	teNER oona abeREEya
breakfast	el desayuno	el dessaYOOno
to do breast-stroke	nadar pecho	naDAR PEtsho
bride	la novia	la NObya
bridegroom	el novio	el NObyo
bridge	el puente	el PWENte
bright	vivo(a)	BEEbo(a)
to bring up	criar	kreeAR
broad	ancho(a)	ANtsho(a)
brooch	el prendedor	el prendeDOR
brother	el hermano	el erMAno
brown	marrón	maRRRON
brown hair	el pelo castaño	el PElo kassTANyo
bruise	el moretón	el moreTONN
brush (for painting)	el pincel	el peenSSEL
brush	el cepillo	el ssePEElyo
toothbrush	el cepillo de dientes	el ssePEElyo de DYENtess
to brush your hair	cepillarse el pelo	ssepeeLYARsse el PElo
to brush your teeth	lavarse los dientes	laBARsse loss DYENtess
Brussels sprout	la col de Bruselas	la kol de brooSSElass
bucket	el baldecito	el baldeSSEEto
buffet car	el coche-restaurante	el KOtshe rrrestaooRANte
builder	el albañil	el albanYEEL
building	el edificio	el edeeFEEssyo
bulb (plant)	el bulbo	el BOOLbo
bunch of flowers	el ramo de flores	el RRRAmo de FLOress
burn	la quemadura	la kemaDOOra
bus	el camión	el kaMYONN
	el colectivo	el kolekTEEbo
	el bus	el boos
	la guagua	la GWAgwa
bus stop	la parada de camiones	la paRAda de kaMYONNess
to take the bus	tomar el camión	toMAR el kaMYONN
bush	el arbusto	el arBOOSSto
bustling	animado(a)	aneeMAdo(a)
busy	ocupado(a)	okooPAdo(a)
butcher	el carnicero	el karneeSSEro
butter	la mantequilla	la manteKEElya
butterfly	la mariposa	la mareePOssa
button	el botón	el boTONN
to buy	comprar	komPRAR

C

English	Spanish	Pronunciation
cabbage	la col	la kol
cabin	el camarote	el kamaROte
cage	la jaula	la chaOOla
cake	el pastel	el passTEL
cake store	la pastelería	la passteleREEya
to calculate	hacer cuentas	aSSER KWENtass
calculator	la calculadora	la kalkoolaDOra
calendar	el calendario	el kalenDAryo
calf	la ternera	la terNEra
camel	el camello	el kaMElyo
camera	la máquina fotográfica	la MAkeena fotoGRAfeeka
camper	la caravana	la karaBAna
camping stove	la estufita	la esstooFEEta
campsite	el camping	el KAMpeeng
can	la lata	la LAta
canned food	los productos en lata	loss proDOOKtoss en LAta
Can I help you?	¿Qué desea?	ke deSSEya
Canada	el Canadá	el kanaDA
canary	el canario	el kaNAryo
candle	la vela	la BEla
canoe	la canoa	la kaNOa
cap	la gorra	la GOrrra
capital letter	la mayúscula	la maYOOSSkoola
capital town or city	la capital	la kapeeTAL
to capsize	volcarse	bolKARsse
captain	el capitán	el kapeeTAN
car	el coche	el KOtshe
card	la tarjeta	la tarCHEta
postcard	la postal	la posTAL
credit card	la tarjeta de crédito	la tarCHEta de KREdeeto
playing card	la carta	la KARta
to play cards	jugar a las cartas	chooGAR a lass KARtass
cardigan	la chaqueta de punto	la tshaKEta de POONto
careful	cuidadoso(a)	kweedaDOsso(a)
careless	descuidado(a)	desskweeDAdo(a)
cargo, load	la carga	la KARga
carnation	el clavel	el klaBEL
carol	el villancico	el beelyanSSEEko
carpet, rug	la alfombra	la alFOMbra
wall-to-wall carpet	la alfombra de pared a pared	la alFOMbra de paRED a paRED
carriage	el vagón	el baGONN
carrot	la zanahoria	la ssanaOrya
to carry	llevar	lyeBAR
cart (for baggage or in supermarket)	el carrito	el karRREEto
cashier (m)	el cajero	el kaCHEro
cashier (f)	la cajera	la kaCHEra
cassette	el cassette	el kaSSET
cassette recorder	la grabadora	la grabaDOra
cat	el gato	el GAto
to catch	agarrar	agaRRRAR
to catch a fish	pescar un pez	pessCAR oon pess

English	Spanish	Pronunciation
cathedral	la catedral	la kateDRAL
cauliflower	la coliflor	la koleeFLOR
to celebrate	celebrar	sseleBRAR
cellar	el sótano	el SSOtano
cello	el violonchelo	el beeolonTSHElo
to play the cello	tocar el violonchelo	toKAR el beeolonTSHElo
cemetery	el cementerio	el ssemenTERyo
centimeter	el centímetro	el ssenTEEmetro
center	el centro	el SSENtro
chair	la silla	la SSEElya
chalk	la tiza	la TEEssa
change	el cambio	el KAMbyo
Have you any change?	¿Tienes cambio?	TYEness KAMbyo
channel (TV, radio)	el canal	el kaNAL
to chase	perseguir	persseGEER
to chat	charlar	tsharLAR
check	la cuenta	la KWENta
check-in desk	el mostrador	el mostraDOR
checkout	la caja	la CAcha
cheek	la mejilla	la meCHEElya
cheerful	alegre	aLEgre
cheese	el queso	el KEsso
chemistry	la química	la KEEmeeka
check	el cheque	el TSHEke
to write a check	hacer un cheque	aSSER un TSHEke
check book	la chequera	la tsheKEra
checkers	las damas	lass DAmass
to play checkers	jugar a las damas	chooGAR a lass DAmass
cherry	la cereza	la sseREssa
chess	el ajedrez	el acheDRESS
to play chess	jugar al ajedrez	chooGAR al acheDRESS
chest	el pecho	el PEtsho
chick peas	los garbanzos	loss garBANssoss
chicken	el pollo	el POlyo
child	el niño, el hijo	el NEENyo, el EEcho
childhood	la niñez	la neenYESS
chimney	la chimenea	la tsheemeNEya
chin	el mentón	el menTON
China	China	TSHEEna
chocolate	el chocolate	el tshokoLAte
choir	el coro	el KOro
Christmas	las Navidades	lass nabeeDAdess
Christmas Day	el Día de Navidad	el DEEya de nabeeDAD
Merry Christmas!	¡Feliz Navidad!	feLEESS nabeeDAD
Christmas tree	el árbol de Navidad	el ARbol de nabeeDAD
chrysanthemum	el crisantemo	el kreessanTEmo
church	la iglesia	la eeGLESSya
circle	el círculo	el SSEERkoolo
to clap	aplaudir	aplaooDEER
classical music	la música clásica	la MOOseeka KLAseeka
classroom	la clase	la KLAsse
claw	la garra	la GArrra
clean	limpio(a)	LEEMpyo(a)
climate	el clima	el KLEEma
to climb	trepar	trePAR
to climb (mountain climbing)	escalar	esskaLAR
to climb a tree	subirse a un árbol	sooBEERse a oon ARbol
climber	el alpinista	el alpeeNEESSta
clock	el reloj	el rrreLOCH
to close	cerrar	sseRRRAR
clothes, clothing	ropa (f)	la RRROpa
clothes line	la cuerda de la ropa	la KWERda de la RRROpa
clothes pin	el broche	el BROtshe
cloud	la nube	la NOObe
coat	el abrigo	el abREEgo
coatroom	el guardarropa	el guardaRRROpa
cod	el bacalao	el bakaLAo
coffee	el café	el caFE
coffee pot	la cafetera	la kafeTEra
coin	la moneda	la moNEda
coin purse	el monedero	el moneDEro
cold	frío(a)	FREEyo(a)
It's cold.	Hace frío.	Asse FREEyo
cold water	el agua fría	el Agwa FREEya
to collect stamps	coleccionar estampillas	kolekssyoNAR esstampEELyass
collection	la colección	la kolekSSYONN
collection times (mail)	las horas de recogida	lass ORass de rrrekoCHEEda
collision	el choque	el TSHoke
color	el color	el koLOR
comb	el peine	el PEYne
to comb your hair	peinarse	peyNARsse
comic (book)	el comic	el KOmeek
complexion	la tez	la tess
computer	la computadora	la kompootaDOra
computer studies	la computación	la compootaSSYONN
condiments	las especias	lass essPEssyass
conductor (orchestra)	el director de orquesta	el deerekTOR de orKESSta
cone	el cono	el KOno
to congratulate	felicitar	feleesseeTAR
Congratulations!	¡Felicidades!	feleesseeDAdess
continent	el continente	el konteeNENte
to cook	cocinar	kosseeNAR
cookie	la galletita	la galyeTEEta
corner	la esquina	la essKEEna
to cost	costar	kossTAR
It costs...	Cuesta...	KWESSta
crib	la cuna	la KOOna
cottage	la cabaña	la kaBAnya
cotton	el algodón	el algoDONN
made of cotton	de algodón	de algoDONN
counter	el mostrador	el mosstraDOR
country	el país	el paEESS
countryside	el campo	el KAMpo
course	el curso	el KOORsso
cousin (m)	el primo	el PREEmo
cousin (f)	la prima	la PREEma
cow	la vaca	la BAka
cowshed	el establo	el essTAblo
crab	el cangrejo	el kanGREcho
to do the crawl	nadar crol	naDAR krol
crayon	el crayón	el kraYONN
cream	la crema	la KREma
credit card	la tarjeta de crédito	la tarCHEta de KREdeeto
crew	la tripulación	la treepoolaSSYONN
to cross the street	cruzar la calle	crooSSAR la KAlye
crossing (sea)	la travesía	la trabeSSEEya

crowd	el grupo de gente	el GROOpo de CHENte
to cry	llorar	lyoRAR
cup	la taza	la TAssa
cupboard	la alacena	la alaSSEna
to cure	curar	kooRAR
curly	rizado(a)	rrreeSSAdo(a)
curly hair	el pelo rizado	el PElo rrreeSSAdo
curtain	la cortina	la korTEEna
customer (m)	el cliente	el kleeYENte
customer (f)	la clienta	la kleeYENta
customs	la aduana	la adooWAna
customs officer	el aduanero	el adoowaNEro
cut (wound)	la cortadura	la kortaDOOra

D

daisy	la margarita	la margaREEta
to dance	bailar	baeeLAR
dance floor	la pista de baile	la PEESSta de BAeele
dark (color)	oscuro(a)	ossKOOro(a)
dark (complexion)	moreno(a)	moREno(a)
date	la fecha	la FEtsha
daughter	la hija	la EEcha
only daughter	la hija única	la EEcha OOneeka
dawn	el amanecer	el amaneSSER
day, daytime	el día	el DEEya
the day after tomorrow	pasado mañana	paSSAdo manYAna
the day before yesterday	anteayer	anteaYER
Dear...	Querido(a)...	keREEdo(a)
Dear Sir/Madam	Muy señor mío/	mooy ssenYOR MEEyo/
	Estimada señora	essteeMAda ssenYOra
death	la muerte	la MWERte
December	diciembre	deeSSYEMbre
deck	la cubierta	la kooBYERta
deep	profundo(a)	proFOONdo(a)
delicatessen	la fiambrería	la fyambreREEya
delicious	riquísimo(a)	rrreeKEEsseemo(a)
to deliver	entregar	entreGAR
democratic	democrático(a)	demoKRAteeko(a)
dentist (m/f)	el/la dentista	el/la denTEESSta
department (in store)	el departamento	el departaMENto
department store	los grandes almacenes	loss GRANdess almaSSEness
Departures	salidas (f. pl)	ssaLEEdass
desert	el desierto	el dessyERto
designer (m)	el diseñador	el deessenyaDOR
designer (f)	la diseñadora	la deessenyaDOra
dessert	el postre	el POSStre
to dial the number	marcar el número	marKAR el NOOmero
diary	la agenda	la aCHENda
to die	morirse	moREERsse
different	diferente	deefeRENte
difficult	difícil	deeFEEsseel
to dig	cavar	kaBAR
dining room	el comedor	el komeDOR
dinner	la cena	la SSEna
dirty	sucio(a)	SSOOssyo(a)

district	el distrito	el deessTREEto
to dive	tirarse	teeRARsse
to divide	dividir	deebeeDEER
divided by	dividido por	deebeeDEER por
diving board	el trampolín	el trampoLEEn
DJ	el disc jockey	el deesk djoKEY
to do	hacer	aSSER
Do Not Enter	Prohibido el paso	proeeBEEdo el PAsso
to do back-stroke	nadar de espalda	naDAR de essPALda
to do breast-stroke	nadar pecho	naDAR PEtsho
to do the crawl	nadar crol	naDAR krol
to do the gardening	cuidar el jardín	kweeDAR el charDEEN
to do the laundry	lavar la ropa	laBAR la RRROpa
to do the shopping	hacer las compras	aSSER lass KOMprass
dock, quay	el muelle	el mooWElye
doctor (m)	el médico	el MEdeeko
doctor (f)	la médica	la MEdeeka
dog	el perro	el PErrro
dog house	la perrera	la peRRREra
doll	la muñeca	la mooNYEca
donkey	el burro	el BOOrrro
donut	el buñuelo	el booNYWElo
door	la puerta	la PWERta
front door	la puerta de entrada	la PWERta de enTRAda
doorbell	el timbre	el TEEMbre
doormat	el felpudo	el felPOOdo
double room	la habitación doble	la abeetaSSYONN DOble
down	abajo	aBAcho
downstairs	abajo	aBAcho
to go downstairs	bajar	baCHAR
downtown	el centro	el SSENtro
dragonfly	la libélula	la leeBEloola
to draw the curtains	descorrer las cortinas	desskoRRRER lass corTEEnass
to dream	soñar	ssonYAR
dress	el vestido	el bessTEEdo
to get dressed	vestirse	bessTEERsse
dressing gown	la bata	la BAta
to drink	beber	beBER
to drive	manejar	maneCHAR
driver (m)	el conductor	el kondookTOR
driver (f)	la conductora	la kondookTOra
to drop	dejar caer	deCHAR kaER
to dry	secar	sseKAR
to dry your hair	secarse el pelo	sseKARsse el PElo
to dry yourself	secarse	sseKARsse
duck	el pato	el PAto
dull	apagado(a)	apaGAdo(a)
dustman	el basurero	el bassooREro
duty-free shop	la tienda libre de impuestos	la TYENda LEEbre de eemPWESStoss

E

eagle	el águila (f)	el Ageela
ear	la oreja	la oREcha
earrings	los aretes	loss aREtess
east	el este	el ESSte
Easter	Pascua	PASSkwa

113

easy	fácil	FAsseel
to eat	comer	koMER
to have eaten	haber comido	aBER komEEdo
well	bien	byen
egg	el huevo	el WEbo
eight	ocho	Otsho
8 in the morning,	las ocho de la	lass Otsho de la
8 a.m.	mañana	manYAna
8 in the evening,	las ocho de la	lass Otsho de la
8 p.m.	tarde	TARde
eighteen	dieciocho	dyesseeOtsho
eighty	ochenta	oTSHENta
elastic	la cinta elástica	la SSEENta eLASSteeka
elbow	el codo	el KOdo
election	las elecciones	lass elekseeOness
electric razor	la maquinilla eléctrica	la makeeNEElya eLEKtreeka
electricity	la electricidad	la elektreesseeDAD
elephant	el elefante	el eleFANte
eleven	once	ONsse
emergency	la emergencia	la emerCHENssya
emergency room	urgencias	oorCHENssyass
to employ someone	emplear a alguien	empleAR a alGYEN
employee (m)	el empleado	el empleAdo
employee (f)	la empleada	la empleAda
empty	vacío(a)	baSSEEyo(a)
to empty	vaciar	bassyAR
I enclose...	Adjunto...	adCHOONto
end of course	el fin de curso	el feen de KOORsso
to get engaged	comprometerse	compromeTERsse
engine	la máquina	la MAkeena
English (language or subject)	el inglés	el eenGLESS
to enjoy, to like	gustarle a uno	goossTARle a OOno
Enjoy your meal.	¡Que aproveche!	ke aproBEtshe
to enjoy yourself	divertirse	deeberTEERsse
enormous	enorme	eNORme
Do Not Enter (road sign)	Prohibido el paso	proeeBEEdo el PAsso
entrance	la entrada	la enTRAda
envelope	el sobre	el SSObre
Equator	el ecuador	el ekwaDOR
eraser	la goma	la GOma
escalator	la escalera automática	la eskaLEra aootoMAteeca
Europe	Europa	eooROpa
evening	la tarde	la TARde
8 in the evening, 8 p.m.	las ocho de la tarde	lass Otsho de la TARde
this evening	ésta tarde	ESSta TARde
exam	el examen	el ekSSAmen
to fail an exam	no aprobar	no aproBAR
to pass an exam	aprobar	aproBAR
to take an exam	dar un examen	dar un ekSSAmen
to exchange money	cambiar dinero	kamBYAR deeNEro
exchange rate	el tipo de cambio	el TEEpo de KAMbyo
to exercise	entrenarse	entreNARsse
exhibition	la exposición	la ekssposseeSSYONN
exit	la salida	la ssaLEEda
expensive.	caro(a)	KAro(a)
It's expensive.	Es caro.	ess KAro
eye	el ojo	el Ocho

F

fabric	la tela	la TEla
face	la cara	la KAra
factory	la fábrica	la FAbreeka
to fail an exam	no aprobar	no aproBAR
to faint	desmayarse	desmaYARsse
fair (complexion)	blanco(a)	BLANko(a)
fall	el otoño	el oTOnyo
to fall asleep	dormirse	dorMEERsse
false	falso(a)	FALsso(a)
family	la familia	la faMEELya
famous	famoso(a)	faMOsso(a)
far	lejos	LEchoss
far away from	lejos de	LEchoss de
How far is...?	¿A qué distancia está...?	a ke deesTANssya essTA
fare	el precio del viaje	el PREssyo del beeAche
farm	la granja	la GRANcha
farmer (m)	el granjero	el granCHEro
farmer (f)	la granjera	la granCHEra
farmhouse	la case de campo	la KAssa de KAMpo
farmyard	el patio	el PAtyo
fashionable	de moda	de MOda
fast	rápido(a)	RRRApeedo(a)
Fasten your seatbelts.	¡Abrocharse el cinturón!	abroCHARssee el sseentooRONN
fat	gordo(a)	GORdo(a)
father	el padre	el PAdre
faucet	el grifo	el GREEfo
feather	la pluma	la PLOOma
February	febrero	feBREro
to feed	dar de comer	dar de koMER
to feel better	sentirse mejor	ssenTEERsse meCHOR
to feel ill	sentirse mal	ssenTEERsse mal
ferry	el ferry	el FErrree
to fetch	traer	traER
field	el campo	el KAMpo
field (soccer)	el campo de fútbol	el KAMpo de FOOTbol
fifteen	quince	KEENsse
the fifth (date)	el cinco	el SSEENko
fifty	cincuenta	sseenKWENta
to fill	llenar	lyeNAR
to fill up with gas	llenar de gasolina	lyeNAR de gassoLEEna
to have a filling	empastarse un diente	empassTARsse un DYENte
film (in camera)	la película	la peLEEkoola
It's fine.	Hace buen tiempo.	Asse bwen TYEMpo
finger	el dedo	el DEdo
fire	el fuego	el FWEgo
fire engine	el camión de bomberos	el kameeONN de bomBEross
fireman	el bombero	el bomBEro
fireplace	la chimenea	la tsheemeNEya
to fire someone	despedir a alguien	desspeDEER a ALgyen
fire station	la estación de bomberos	la esstaSSYONN de bomBEross
the first	el primero	el preeMEro
first class	primera clase	preeMEra KLAsse
first floor	planta baja	PLANta BAcha

first name	el nombre de pila	el NOMbre de PEEla
fish	el pescado	el pesKAdo
fish bowl	la pecera	la peSSEra
fishing boat	el bote de pesca	el BOte de PEsska
fish market	la pescadería	la pesskadeREEya
to keep fit	mantenerse en forma	manteNERsse en FORma
five	cinco	SSEENko
five past ten	las diez y cinco	lass dyess ee SSEENko
flag	la bandera	la banDEra
flavor, taste	el sabor	el ssaBOR
to float	flotar	floTAR
flock	el rebaño	el rrreBANyo
flood	la inundación	la eenoondaSSYONN
floor	el suelo	el SWElo
first floor	planta baja	PLANta BAcha
second floor	primer piso	preeMER PEEsso
third floor	segundo piso	seGOONdo PEEsso
florist	la floristería	la floreessteREEya
flour	la harina	la aREEna
flower	la flor	la flor
bunch of flowers	el ramo de flores	el RRRAmo de FLOress
wild flowers	las flores silvestres	lass FLOress seelBESStress
fly	la mosca	la MOSSka
to fly	volar	boLAR
fog	la niebla	la NYEbla
It's foggy.	Hay niebla.	aee NYEbla
to follow	seguir	seGEER
to be fond of	tenerle cariño a	teNERle kaREENyo a
foot	el pie	el pyE
forget-me-nots	las nomeolvides	lass nomeolBEEdess
fork (table)	el tenedor	el teneDOR
fork (gardening)	la horquilla	la orKEEya
form	el formulario	el formooLAryo
forty	cuarenta	kwaRENta
forward	hacia adelante	Assya adeLANte
foundation cream	la base	la BAsse
four	cuatro	KWAtro
fourteen	catorce	kaTORse
the fourth (date)	el cuatro	el KWAtro
fox	el zorro	el SSOrrro
fraction	la fracción	la frakSSYONN
France	Francia	FRANssya
freckles	las pecas	lass PEkas
freight train	el tren de carga	el tren de KARga
French (language or subject)	el francés	el franSSESS
fresh	fresco(a)	FRESSko(a)
Friday	viernes (m)	BYERness
fridge	la nevera	la neBEra
friend (m)	el amigo	el aMEEgo
friend (f)	la amiga	la aMEEga
friendly	amistoso(a)	ameessTOsso(a)
frightened	asustado(a)	assoossTAdo(a)
frog	la rana	la RRRAna
from	de	de
front door	la puerta de entrada	la PWERta de enTRAda
frost	la escarcha	la essKARtsha
to frown	fruncir el ceño	froonSSEER el SSENyo
frozen food	los congelados	loss koncheLAdoss
fruit	la fruta	la FROOta

fruit juice	el jugo de frutas	el CHOOgo de FROOtass
full	lleno(a)	LYEno(a)
to have fun	divertirse	deeberTEERsse
funeral	el entierro	el enTYErrro
funny	gracioso(a)	grasseeOsso(a)
fur	el pelo	el PElo
furniture	muebles (m. pl)	MWEbless
future	el futuro	el fooTOOro
in the future	en el futuro	en el fooTOOro

G

to gain speed	acelerar	asseleRAR
galaxy	la galaxia	la gaLAKSSya
art gallery	la galería de arte	la galeREEya de ARte
games	los juegos	loss CHWEgoss
gangway	la pasarela	la passaRElla
garage	el garaje	el gaRAche
garden shed	el cobertizo	el coberTEEsso
gardener	el jardinero	el chardeeNEro
to do the gardening	cuidar el jardín	kweeDAR el charDEEN
garlic	el ajo	el Acho
gas	la gasolina	la gassoLEEna
gas cylinder	la bombona	la bomBOna
to fill up with gas	llenar de gasolina	lyeNAR de gassoLEEna
natural gas	el gas	el gass
gas station	la gasolinera	la gassoleeNEra
gate	la tranquera	la tranKEra
generous	generoso(a)	cheneROso(a)
geography	la geografía	la cheograFEEya
geranium	el geranio	el cheRAneo
German (language or subject)	el alemán	el aleMAN
Germany	Alemania	aleMANya
to get dressed	vestirse	bessTEERsse
to get engaged	comprometerse	kompromeTERsse
to get married	casarse	kaSSARsse
to get off (bus or train)	bajarse	baCHARsse
to get on (bus or train)	subirse	sooBEERsse
to get undressed	quitarse la ropa	keeTARsse la RRROpa
to get up	levantarse	lebanTARsse
giraffe	la jirafa	la cheeRAfa
girl	la niña	la NEENya
to give	dar	dar
to give (a present)	regalar	rrregaLAR
glass	el vaso	el BAsso
glasses, spectacles	las gafas	lass GAfass
sunglasses	las gafas de sol	lass GAfass de ssol
gloves	los guantes	loss GWANtess
to go	ir	eer
to go to bed	acostarse	akossTARsse
to go camping	ir de camping	eer de KAMpeeng
to go to the cinema	ir al cine	eer al SSEEne
to go downstairs	bajar	baCHAR
to go fishing	ir de pesca	eer de PESSka
to go mountain climbing	hacer alpinismo	aSSER alpeeNEESmo

to go to a nightclub	ir a una discoteca	eer a OOna deeskoTEka
to go shopping	ir de compras	eer de KOMprass
to go straight	seguir todo derecho	sseGEER TOdo deREtsho
to go to the supermarket	ir al supermercado	eer al soopermerKAdo
to go upstairs	subir	ssooBEER
to go on vacation	ir de vacaciones	eer de bakaSSYOness
to go for a walk	dar un paseo	dar un paSSEyo
to go window-shopping	ir de escaparates	eer de esskapaRAtess
to go to work	ir a trabajar	eer a trabaCHAR
goal	el gol	el gol
goalkeeper	el arquero	el arKEro
goat	la cabra	la KAbra
gold	el oro	el Oro
made of gold	de oro	de Oro
goldfish	el pez de colores	el pess de koLOress
golf club	el palo de golf	el PAlo de golf
to play golf	jugar al golf	chooGAR al golf
good	bueno(a)	BWEno(a)
Goodbye.	¡Adiós!	adeeOSS
good-looking	guapo(a)	GWApo
Good luck!	¡Buena suerte!	BWEna SSWERte
Good morning!	¡Buenos días!	BWEnoss DEEyass
Good night!	¡Hasta mañana!	ASta manYAna
It's a good value.	Está a buen precio.	essTA a bwen PREssyo
It tastes good.	Está muy rico.	essTA mooy RRREEko
goose	el ganso	el GANsso
gorilla	el gorila	el goREEla
government	el gobierno	el goBYERno
grade school	la escuela primaria	la essKWEla preeMArya
grammar	la gramática	la graMAteeka
granddaughter	la nieta	la NYEta
grandfather	el abuelo	el aBWElo
grandmother	la abuela	la aBWEla
grandson	el nieto	el NYEto
grape	la uva	la OOba
grass	la hierba	la YERba
gray	gris	greess
Great Britain	Gran Bretaña	gran breTANya
green	verde	BERde
greenhouse	el invernadero	el eenbernaDEro
grocery bag	la bolsa	la bolSSEEta
grocery store	la tienda de comestibles	la TYENda de komessTEEbles
to growl	gruñir	groonYEER
guard	el guarda	el GWARda
guest (m)	el invitado	el eenbeeTAdo
guest house, boarding house	la pensión	la penSYONN
guinea pig	el conejillo de Indias	el koneCHEElyo de EENdyass
guitar	guitarra	la geeTArrra
to play the guitar	tocar la guitarra	toKAR la geeTArrra
gymnastics	la gimnasia	la cheemNASSya

H

hail	el granizo	el graNEEsso
to hail a taxi	parar un taxi	paRAR oon TAKsee
hair	el pelo	el PElo
to have ... color hair	tener el pelo ...	teNER el PElo
hairdryer	el secador	el ssekaDOR
hake	la merluza	la merLOOssa
a half	medio	MEdyo
half a kilo	medio kilo	MEdyo KEElo
half a liter	medio litro	MEdyo LEEtro
half past ten	las diez y media	lass dyess ee MEdya
half slip	las enaguas	lass enAgwass
ham	el jamón	el chaMONN
hammer	el martillo	el marTEElyo
hamster	el hámster	el AMster
hand	la mano	la MAno
hand luggage	el equipaje de mano	el ekeePAche de MAno
to hang on to	colgarse de	kolGARsse de
to hang up (telephone)	colgar	kolGAR
happy	feliz	feLEESS
to be happy	ser feliz	sser feLEESS
Happy New Year!	¡Feliz Año Nuevo!	feLEESS ANyo NWEbo
hard	duro(a)	DOOro(a)
hard-working	trabajador(a)	trabachaDOR(a)
to harvest	cosechar	kosseTSHAR
hat	el sombrero	el ssomBREro
to have	tener	teNER
to have a beard	tener barba	teNER BARba
to have blond hair	tener el pelo rubio	teNER el PElo ROObyo
to have a breakdown (vehicle)	tener una avería	teNER OOna abeREEya
Have you any change?	¿Tienes cambio?	TYEness KAMbyo
to have a cold	estar resfriado	essTAR rrressfreeAdo
to have ... color hair	tener el pelo ...	teNER el PElo
to have eaten well	haber comido bien	aBER coMEEdo byen
to have a filling	empastarse un diente	empassTARsse oon DYENte
to have a flat tire	tener una rueda pinchada	teNER oona RWEda peenTSHAda
to have fun	divertirse	deeberTEERsse
to have a headache	tener dolor de cabeza	teNER doLOR de kaBEssa
to have a mustache	tener bigote	teNER beeGOte
to have red hair	ser pelirrojo(a)	sser peliRRROcho
to have a stomach ache	tener dolor de estómago	teNER doLOR de essTOmago
to have straight hair	tener el pelo lacio	teNER el PElo LAssyo
to have a temperature	tener fiebre	teNER FYEbre
to have toothache	tener dolor de muelas	teNER doLOR de MWElass
Having a lovely time.	Pasándolo muy bien.	paSSANdolo mooy byen
hay, haystack	el heno	el Eno

head	la cabeza	la kaBEssa
to have a	tener dolor de	teNER doLOR de
headache	cabeza	kaBEssa
headband	la cinta	la SSINta
headlight	el faro	el FAro
headlines	los titulares	loss teetooLAress
headphones	los auriculares	loss aooreekooLAress
healthy	sano(a)	SSAno(a)
heavy	pesado	peSSAdo(a)
to be heavy	pesar mucho	peSSAR MOOtsho
hedgehog	el erizo	el eREEsso
heel	el talón	el taLONN
height	la altura	la alTOOra
Hello	¡Hola!	Ola
to help	ayudar	ayooDAR
Help yourself.	¡Sírvete!	SEERbete
Can I help you?	¿Qué desea?	ke deSSEa
hen	la gallina	la gaLYEEna
henhouse	el gallinero	el galyeeNEro
hero	el héroe	el Eroe
heroine	la heroína	la eroEEna
to hide	esconderse	esskonDERsse
high school	el colegio	el koLEchyo
hill	el cerro	el SSErrro
hippopotamus	el hipopótamo	el eepoPOtamo
His name is...	Se llama...	sse LYAma
history	la historia	la eessTOrya
hold (ship)	la bodega	la boDEga
to hold	sostener	sossteNER
honey	la miel	la myel
honeymoon	el viaje de novios	el BYAche de NObyoss
hook (fishing)	el anzuelo	el anSSWElo
horn	la bocina	la boSSEEna
horse	el caballo	el kaBAlyo
horse racing	las carreras de caballos	lass kaRRRErass de kaBAlyoss
hose	las medias largas	lass MEdyass LARgass
hospital	el hospital	el osspeeTAL
hot	caliente	kaLYENte
hot water	el agua (f) caliente	el Agwa kaLYENte
I'm hot.	Tengo calor.	TENgo kaLOR
hotel	el hotel	el oTEL
to stay in a hotel	quedarse en un hotel	keDARsse en oon oTEL
hour	la hora	la Ora
house	la casa	la KAssa
How are you?	¿Qué tal?	ke tal
How far is...?	¿A qué distancia está...?	a ke deessTANssya essTA
How much...?	¿Cuánto...?	KWANto
How much do I owe you?	¿Cuánto es?	KWANto ess
How much is...?	¿Cuánto cuesta...?	KWANto KWESSta
How old are you?	¿Cuántos años tienes?	KWANtoss ANyos TYEness
hump	la giba	la CHEEba
a hundred	cien	ssyen
	ciento	SSYENto
to be hungry	tener hambre	teNER AMbre
to hurry	apurarse	apooRARsse
husband	el marido	el maREEdo

I

I agree	De acuerdo	de aKWERdo
I am sending... separately.	Te mando por separado...	te MANdo por ssepaRAdo
I'd like...	Querría...	keRRREEya
I enclose...	Adjunto...	adCHOONto
I'll call you back.	Te llamo más tarde.	te LYAmo mass TARde
I'm nineteen	Tengo diecinueve años	TENgo dyesseeNWEbe ANyoss
ice cream	el helado	el eLAdo
icicle	el carámbano	el kaRAMbano
to feel ill	sentirse mal	ssenTEERsse mal
important	importante	eemporTANte
In (sports)	Dentro	DENtro
in	en	en
in focus	enfocado	enfoKAdo
in front of	delante de	deLANte de
in the future	en el futuro	en el fooTOOro
India	la India	la EEndya
ingredient	el ingrediente	el eengreDYENte
injection	la inyección	la eenyekSSYONN
instrument	el instrumento	el eensstrooMENto
intercity train	el tren interurbano	el tren eenteroorBAno
intercom	el altoparlante	el altoparLANte
interesting	interesante	eentereSSANte
to interview	entrevistar	entrebeessTAR
into	dentro	DENtro
to introduce	presentar	pressenTAR
to invite	invitar	eenbeeTAR
to iron	planchar	planTSHAR
Is the tip included?	¿Está incluido el servicio?	essTA eenklooEEdo el sserBEEssyo
It costs...	Cuesta...	KWESSta
It's cold.	Hace frío.	Asse FREEyo
It's dark.	Es de noche.	ess de NOtshe
It's quite expensive.	Es bastante caro.	ess bassTANte KAro
It's fine.	Hace buen tiempo.	Asse bwen TYEMpo
It's foggy.	Hay niebla.	Ay NYEbla
It's getting dark.	Oscurece.	oscooREsse
It's getting light.	Amanece.	amaNEsse
It's a good value.	Está a buen precio.	essTA a bwen PREssyo
It's... (on phone)	Soy...	ssoy
It's light.	Es de día.	ess de DEEya
It's 1 o'clock.	Es la una.	ess la OOna
It's raining.	Llueve.	lyooEba
It's ready.	Está listo.	essTA LEESSto
It's snowing.	Nieva.	NYEba
It's 3 o'clock.	Son las tres.	sson lass TRESS
It's windy.	Hace viento.	Asse BYENto
It tastes good.	Está muy rico.	essTA mooy REEko
It was lovely to hear from you.	Me encantó tener noticias tuyas.	me enkanTO teNER noTEEssyass TOOyass
Italy	Italia	eeTALya

J

jacket	la chaqueta	la tshaKEta
jam	la mermelada	la mermeLAda

janitor (m)	el portero	el porTEro
janitor (f)	la portera	la porTEra
January	enero	eNEro
Japan	el Japón	el chaPONN
jeans	los vaqueros	loss baKEross
jewelry	las joyas	lass CHOyass
job, profession	la profesión	la profeSSYONN
to jog	hacer fúting	aSSER FOOteen
to join	asociarse	assosseeARsse
journalist (m/f)	el/la periodista	el/la pereeoDEESSta
judge	el juez	el CHWEss
July	julio	CHOOLyo
sweater	el suéter	el SWEter
June	junio	CHOONyo
jungle	la selva	la SSELba

K

kangaroo	el canguro	el kanGOOro
to keep an eye on	vigilar	beecheeLAR
to keep fit	mantenerse en forma	manteNERsse en FORma
keeper	el guardián	el gwardeeANN
keyboard	el teclado	el teKLAdo
kilo	el kilo	el KEElo
A kilo of...	Un kilo de...	oon KEElo de
Half a kilo of...	Medio kilo de...	MEdyo KEElo de
kindergarten	la guardería	la gwardeREEya
at kindergarten	en la guardería	en la gwardeREEya
to kiss	dar un beso	dar oon BEsso
kitchen	la cocina	la koSSEna
kitten	el gatito	el gaTEEto
knee	la rodilla	la rrroDEElya
to kneel down	arrodillarse	arrrodeeLYARsse
to be kneeling	estar de rodillas	essTAR de rrroDEElyass
panties	los calzones	loss calSSOnes
knife	el cuchillo	el kooTSHEElyo
to knit	tejer	teCHER
knitting needles	las agujas	lass AGOOchass
to knock over	volcar	bolKAR

L

label	la etiqueta	la eteeKEta
labor union	el sindicato	el seendeeKAto
ladder	la escalera	la esskaLEra
lake	el lago	el LAgo
lamb	el cordero	el korDEro
lamp	la lámpara	la LAMpara
to land	aterrizar	aterrreeSSAR
landlady	la dueña	la dooEnya
landlord	el dueño	el dooEnyo
landscape	el paisaje	el paeeSSAche
large	grande	GRANde
last	último(a)	OOLteemo(a)
last night	anoche	aNOtshe
to be late	llevar retraso	lyeBAR rrreTRAsso
to arrive late	llegar tarde	lyeGAR TARde
	estar demorado	essTAR demoRAdo
Latin America	América Latina	aMEreeka laTEEna
to laugh	reírse	rrreEERse
to do the laundry	lavar la ropa	laBAR la RRROpa

lawn	el césped	el SSESSped
lawnmower	la cortadora de césped	la kortaDOra de SSESSped
lawyer (m)	el abogado	el aboGAdo
lawyer (f)	la abogada	la aboGAda
to lay eggs	poner huevos	poNER WEboss
to lay the table	poner la mesa	poNER la MEssa
lazy	perezoso(a)	pereSSOsso(a)
leader (m/f)	el/la líder	el/la LEEder
leaf	la hoja	la Ocha
to lean on	apoyarse en	apoYARsse en
to learn	aprender	aPRENder
to leave	dejar	deCHAR
on the left	a la izquierda	a la eessKYERda
left side	el lado izquierdo	el LAdo eessKYERdo
left wing	de izquierda	de eessKYERda
leg	la pierna	la PYERna
leg of lamb	la pierna de cordero	la PYERna de korDEro
lemon	el limón	el leeMONN
length	el largo	el LARgo
lesson	la lección	la lekSSYONN
letter	la carta	la KARta
letter of alphabet	la letra	la LEtra
lettuce	la lechuga	la leTSHOOga
library	la biblioteca	la beebleeoTEka
license plate	la matrícula	la maTREEkoola
to lie down	acostarse	acossTARsse
life	la vida	la BEEda
lifeguard	el vigilante de playa	el beecheeLANte de PLAya
lift	el ascensor	el assenSSOR
light (weight)	ligero	leeCHEro(a)
to be light	ser liviano	sser leebeeAno
light	la luz	la LOOSS
It's getting light.	Amanece.	amaNEsse
It's light.	Es de día.	ess de DEEya
lightning	los relámpagos	loss rrrelAMpagoss
I'd like...	Querría...	keRRRREEya
liner	el trasatlántico	el trassatLANteeko
lion	el león	el leONN
lip	el labio	el LAbyo
lipstick	el lápiz	el LApeess
list	la lista	la LEESSta
to make a list	hacer una lista	aSSER oona LEESSta
to listen	escuchar	esskooTSHAR
to listen to music	escuchar música	esskooTSHAR MOOsseeka
to listen to the radio	escuchar la radio	esskooTSHAR la RRRAdyo
liter	el litro	el LEEtro
half a liter	medio litro	MEdyo LEEtro
little	pequeño(a)	peKENyo(a)
to live	vivir	beeBEER
to live in a house	vivir en una casa	beeBEER en oona KAssa
lively	animado(a)	aneeMAdo(a)
living room	la sala de estar	la SSAla de essTAR
to load	cargar	karGAR
local ticket (in city)	el boleto urbano	el boLEto oorBAno
long	largo(a)	LARgo(a)
to look for	buscar	boossKAR
Look forward to seeing you soon.	Deseando verte pronto.	desseANdo BErte PRONto

loose	suelto(a)	SWELto
to lose	perder	perDER
loudspeaker	el altoparlante	el altoparLANte
to love	querer a	keRER a
Love from...	Un abrazo de...	oon aBRAsso de
(end of letter)		nabeeDAD
luck	la suerte	la SSWERte
Good luck!	¡Buena suerte!	BWEna SSWERte
luggage rack	el portaequipajes	el portaekeePAchess
lullaby	la canción de	la kanSSYONN de
	cuna	KOOna
lunch	el almuerzo	el alMWERsso
lunch hour	la hora de comer	la Ora de koMER
to be lying down	estar acostado(a)	essTAR
		akossTAdo(a)

M

made of gold	de oro	de Oro
made of metal	de metal	de meTAL
made of plastic	de plástico	de PLASSteeko
made of silver	de plata	de PLAta
magazine	la revista	la rrreBEESSta
mail	el correo	el koRRREo
airmail	por avión	por aBYONN
mailbox	el buzón	el booSSONN
mailman	el cartero	el karTEro
return mail	a vuelta de correo	a BWELta de
		koRRREo
main course	el plato principal	el PLAto
		preennsseePAL
main road	la carretera	la karrreTEra
to make	hacer	aSSER
to make a list	hacer una lista	aSSER oona
		LEESSta
to make a	hacer una	aSSER oona
telephone call	llamada	lyaMAda
man	el hombre	el OMbre
map	el mapa	el MApa
March	marzo	MARsso
margarine	la margarina	la margaREEna
market	el mercado	el merKAdo
market stall	el puesto	el PWESSto
marriage	el casamiento	el kassaMYENto
to get married	casarse	kaSSARsse
mascara	el rímel	el RRREEmel
math	las matemáticas	lass mateMAteekass
May	mayo	MAyo
meadow	el prado	el PRAdo
to measure	medir	meDEER
meat	la carne	la KARne
mechanic (m)	el mecánico	el meKAneeko
media	los medios de	loss MEdyoss de
	comunicación	komooneeka-
		SSYONN
medium	mediano	meDYAno
(clothes size)		
to meet	encontrarse con	enkonTRARsse kon
melon	el melón	el meLONN
to melt	derretir	derrreTEER
member (m/f)	el miembro	el MYEMbro
member of	el diputado	el deepooTAdo
parliament (m)		
member of	la diputada	la deepooTAda
parliament (f)		

to mend	reparar	rrrepaRAR
to mend (clothes)	zurcir	ssoorSSEER
menu	el menú	el meNOO
Merry Christmas!	¡Feliz Navidad!	feLEESS
		nabeeDAD
merry-go-round	la rueda	la rooEda
metal	el metal	el meTAL
made of metal	de metal	de meTAL
meter	el metro	el MEtro
to mew	maullar	maooLYAR
midday	mediodía	medyoDEEya
midnight	medianoche	medyaNOtshe
milk	la leche	la LEtshe
to milk	ordeñar	ordenYAR
a million	un millón	oon meelYONN
mineral water	el agua (f) mineral	el Agwa meeneRAL
minister	el párroco	el PArrroko
minus	menos	MEnoss
minute	el minuto	el meeNOOto
mirror	el espejo	el essPEcho
to miss the train	perder el tren	perDER el TRENN
to mix	mezclar	messKLAR
model (m/f)	el/la modelo	el/la moDElo
mole	el topo	el TOpo
Monday	lunes (m)	LOOness
money	el dinero	el deeNEro
to change money	cambiar dinero	kamBYAR deeNEro
to put money in	meter dinero en	meTER deeNEro en
the bank	el banco	el BANko
to take money out	sacar dinero del	saKAR deeNEro del
of the bank	banco	BANko
monkey	el mono	el MOno
month	el mes	el mess
moon	la luna	la LOOna
moped	el ciclomotor	el sseeklomoTOR
morning	la mañana	la manYAna
8 in the morning,	las ocho de la	lass Otsho de la
8 a.m.	mañana	manYAna
mosquito	el mosquito	el mossKEEto
mother	la madre	la MAdre
motor racing	las carreras de	lass kaRRRErass de
	coches	KOtshess
motorcycle	la motocicleta	la motosseeKLEta
motorway	la autopista	la aootoPEESSta
mountain	la montaña	la monTANya
mountain climbing	el alpinismo	el alpeeNEESSmo
to go mountain	hacer alpinismo	aSSER
climbing		alpeeNEESSmo
mouse	el ratón	el rraTONN
mustache	el bigote	el beeGOte
to have a	tener bigote	teNER beeGOte
mustache		
mouth	la boca	la BOka
to move in	venirse a vivir	beNEERsse a
		beeBEER
to move out	mudarse	mooDARsse
to move/tap your	mover los pies	moBER loss pyess
feet		
movie	la película	la peLEEkoola
movie theater	el cine	el SSEEne
to go to the movies	ir al cine	eer al SSEEne
to mow the lawn	cortar el césped	korTAR el SSESSped
to multiply	multiplicar	moolteepleeKAR
music	la música	la MOOsseeka
classical music	la música clásica	la MOOsseeka
		KLAsseeka
pop music	la música pop	la MOOsseeka pop

English	Spanish	Pronunciation
to paddle	chapotear	tshapoteAR
paint	la pintura	la peenTOOra
to paint	pintar	peenTAR
painter (m)	el pintor	el peenTOR
painter (f)	la pintora	la peenTOra
painting	el cuadro	el KWAdro
pajamas	el pijama	el peeCHAma
pale (color)	claro(a)	KLAro(a)
pants	los pantalones	loss pantaLOness
paper	el papel	el paPEL
paperback	la edición de bolsillo	la edeeSSYONN de bolSEElyo
parcel	el paquete	el paKEte
parents	los padres	loss PAdress
park	el parque	el PARke
to park	estacionar	esstassyoNAR
parking lot	el estacionamiento	el esstassyonaMYENto
No parking	Prohibido estacionar	proeeBEEdo esstassyoNAR
parliament	el parlamento	el parlaMENto
party (celebration)	la fiesta	la FYESSta
party (political)	el partido	el parTEEdo
to pass an exam	aprobar	aproBAR
passenger (m)	el pasajero	el passaCHEro
passenger (f)	la pasajera	la passaCHEra
passport	el pasaporte	el passaPORte
past	el pasado	el paSSAdo
pasta	la pasta	la PASSta
pastry, small tart	el pastelillo	el passteLEElyo
path, footpath	el sendero	el ssenDEro
path, country lane	el camino	el kaMEEno
patient (m/f)	el/la paciente	el/la paSSYENte
pattern	el patrón	el paTRONN
paw	la pata	la PAta
payphone	la cabina de teléfono	la kaBEEna de teLEfono
PE	la gimnasia	la cheemNASSya
peaceful	tranquilo(a)	tranKEElo(a)
peach	el melocotón	el melokoTONN
pear	la pera	la PEra
peas	los chícharos	loss TSHEEtshaross
	las arvejas	lass arBEchass
pedestrian	el peatón	el peaTONN
pedestrian crossing	el paso de peatones	el PAsso de peaTOness
pen	la pluma	la PLOOma
ball point pen	el bolígrafo	el boLEEgrafo
pencil	el lápiz	el LApeess
pencil case	el estuche de lápices	el essTOOtshe de LApeessess
penguin	el pingüino	el peenGWEEno
pepper	la pimienta	la peeMYENta
to perch	posarse	poSSARsse
to perform, act on stage	interpretar	eenterpreTAR
perfume	el perfume	el perFOOme
pharmacy	la farmacia	la farMAssya
photograph	la foto	la FOto
photographer (m)	el fotógrafo	el foTOgrafo
photographer (f)	la fotógrafa	la foTOgrafa
photography	la fotografía	la fotografEEya
physics	la física	la FEEsseeka
piano	el piano	el PYAno
to play the piano	tocar el piano	toKAR el PYAno
to pick, to pick up	recoger	rekoCHER
to pick flowers	recoger flores	rekoCHER FLOress
to pick up the receiver	descolgar	desskolGAR
picnic	el picnic	el PEEKneek
picture book	el libro ilustrado	el LEEbro eelooSTRAdo
pig	el cerdo	el SSERdo
pigeon	la paloma	la paLOma
pill	la pastilla	la passTEElya
pillow	la almohada	la almoAda
pilot	el piloto	el peeLOto
pin	el alfiler	el alfeeLER
pine tree	el pino	el PEEno
pink	rosado(a)	rrroSSAdo(a)
to pitch a tent	montar la tienda de campaña	monTAR la TYENda de kamPANya
pitcher	la jarra	la CHArra
planet	el planeta	el plaNEta
to plant	plantar	planTAR
plastic	el plástico	el PLASSteeko
made of plastic	de plástico	de PLASSteeko
plate	el plato	el PLAto
platform	el andén	el anDENN
play (theater)	la obra de teatro	la Obra de teAtro
to play (games)	jugar	chooGAR
to play (an instrument)	tocar	toKAR
to play cards	jugar a las cartas	chooGAR a lass KARtass
to play checkers	jugar a las damas	chooGAR a lass DAmass
to play chess	jugar al ajedrez	chooGAR al acheDRESS
to play the cello	tocar el violonchelo	toKAR el beeolonCHElo
to play the drums	tocar los tambores	toKAR loss tamBOress
to play golf	jugar al golf	chooGAR al golf
to play the guitar	tocar la guitarra	toKAR la geeTArrra
to play the piano	tocar el piano	toKAR el PYAno
to play soccer	jugar al fútbol	chooGAR al FOOTbol
to play squash	jugar al squash	chooGAR al skwash
to play tennis	jugar al tenis	chooGAR al TEneess
to play the trumpet	tocar la trompeta	toKAR la tromPEta
to play the violin	tocar el violín	toKAR el beeoLEEN
playful	juguetón	choogeTONN
playground	el patio	el PATyo
pleased with	contento(a) con	konTENto(a) kon
to plow	arar	aRAR
plug (electric)	el enchufe	el enTSHOOfe
plug (bath)	el tapón	el taPONN
plum	la ciruela	la sseeRWEla
plumber	el plomero	el ploMEro
plus	más	mass
pocket	el bolsillo	el bolSSElyo
poetry	la poesía	la poeSSEEya
polar bear	el oso blanco	el Osso BLANko
police	la policía	la poleeSSEEya
police car	el coche de policía	el KOtshe de poleeSSEEya
police station	la comisaría	la komeessaREEya
policeman	el policía	el poleeSSEEya
polite	educado(a), bien educado(a)	edooKAdo(a), byen edooKAdo(a)

English	Spanish	Pronunciation
politics	la política	la poLEEteeka
pond	el estanque	el essTANke
pool	el charco	el TCHARko
pop music	la música pop	la MOOsseeka pop
poppy	la amapola	la amaPOla
popular	popular	popooLAR
pork chop	la chuleta de cerdo	la tshooLEta de SSERdo
port	el puerto	el PWERto
porter	el conserje	el konSSERche
porthole	el ojo de buey	el Ocho de bwey
to post	echar al correo	eTSHAR al koRRREo
postcard	la postal	la possTAL
post office	la oficina de correos	la ofeeSSEEna de koRRREoss
potato	la papa	la PApa
to pour	echar	eTSHAR
powerboat	la lancha motora	la LANtsha moTOra
prescription	la receta	la rrreSSEta
present (gift)	el regalo	el rrreGAlo
present (now)	el presente	el preSSENte
president (m)	el presidente	el presseeDENte
president (f)	la presidenta	la presseeDENta
pretty	bonito(a)	boNEEto(a)
price	el precio	el PRESSyo
prime minister (m)	el primer ministro	el preeMER meeNEESStro
prime minister (f)	la primera ministra	la preeMEra meeNEESStra
principal (m)	el director	el deerekTOR
principal (f)	la directora	la deerekTORa
printed	estampado(a)	esstamPAdo(a)
program	el programa	el proGRAma
puddle	el charco	el TSHARko
to pull	tirar	teeRAR
pupil (m)	el alumno	el aLOOMno
pupil (f)	la alumna	la aLOOMna
puppy	el cachorro	el kaTSHOrrro
purple	morado(a)	moRAdo(a)
to purr	ronronear	rrronroneAR
purse	la cartera	la karTEra
to push	empujar	empooCHAR
to put	meter	meTER
to put money in the bank	meter dinero en el banco	meTER deeNEro en el BANko
to put on make-up	maquillarse	makeeLYARsse

Q

English	Spanish	Pronunciation
quarter	un cuarto	oon KWARto
a quarter past ten	las diez y cuarto	lass dyess ee KWARto
a quarter to ten	las diez menos cuarto	lass dyess MEnoss KWARto
quiet	callado(a)	kaLYAdo(a)
quilt	el edredón	el edreDONN

R

English	Spanish	Pronunciation
rabbit	el conejo	el coNEcho
racket	la raqueta	la rrraKEta

English	Spanish	Pronunciation
radiator	el radiador	el rrradeeyaDOR
radio	la radio	la RRRadyo
railway	el ferrocarril	el ferrrokaRRRREEL
rain	la lluvia	la LYOObya
to rain	llover	lyoBER
It's raining.	Llueve.	lyooEbe
rainbow	el arco iris	el ARko EEreess
raincoat	el impermeable	el eempermeAble
raindrop	la gota de lluvia	la GOta de LYOObya
rake	el rastrillo	el rrrassTREELyo
ranger	el guardián	el garDYANN
raspberry	la frambuesa	la framBWEssa
raw	crudo(a)	KROOdo(a)
razor	la máquina de afeitar	la MAkeena de afeyTAR
electric razor	la maquinilla eléctrica	la makeeNEElya eLEKtreeka
to read	leer	leER
to read a book	leer un libro	leER oon LEEbro
to read a story	leer un cuento	leER oon KWENto
It's ready.	Está listo.	essTA LEESSto
receipt	el recibo	el rrreSSEEbo
to receive	recibir	rrresseeBEER
receiver	el auricular	el aooreekooLAR
reception	la recepción	la rrressepSSYONN
recess	el recreo	el reKREo
recipe	la receta	la rrreSSEta
record	el disco	el DEESSko
record player	el tocadiscos	el tokaDEESSkoss
rectangle	el rectángulo	el rrrekTANgoolo
red	rojo(a)	RRROcho(a)
red-haired	pelirrojo(a)	peleeRRROcho(a)
to have red hair	ser pelirrojo(a)	sser peleeRRROcho(a)
reed	el junco	el CHOONko
referee	el árbitro	el ARbeetro
to be related	ser parientes	sser paRYENtess
to repair	reparar	rrrepaRAR
to reserve	reservar	rrresserBAR
to reserve a room	reservar una habitación	rrresserBAR OOna abeetaSSYONN
to reserve a seat	reservar un asiento	rrresserBAR oon aSSYENto
reserved seat	asiento reservado	aSSYENto rrresserBAdo
to rest	descansar	desskanSSAR
restaurant	el restaurante	el rrresstaooRANte
to retire	jubilarse	choobeeLARsse
return mail	a vuelta de correo	a BWELta de koRRREo
rice	al arroz	el aRRROSS
to ride a bicycle	ir en bicicleta	eer en beesseeKLEta
on the right	a la derecha	a la deREtsha
right side	el lado derecho	el lado deREtsho
right wing	de derecha	de deREtsha
ring	el anillo	el aNEElyo
to ring (telephone)	sonar	ssoNAR
to ring the bell	tocar el timbre	toKAR el TEEMbre
ripe	maduro(a)	maDOOro(a)
river	el río	el REEyo
road	la carretera	la karrreTEra
to roar	rugir	rrrooCHEER
rod	la caña	la KANya
roll	el panecillo	el paneSSEElyo
roof	el tejado	el teCHAdo
room (bedroom)	la habitación	la abeetaSSYONN

English	Spanish	Pronunciation
double room	la habitación doble	la abeetaSSYONN DOble
single room	la habitación individual	la abeetaSSYONN eendeebeedooAL
rooster	el gallo	el GAlyo
rose	la rosa	la RRROssa
round trip ticket	el boleto de ida y vuelta	el boLEto de EEDa ee BWELta
to row	remar	rrreMAR
rowboat	el bote de remos	el BOte de RRREmoss
to rub one's eyes	frotarse los ojos	froTARsse loss Ochoss
rubber boots	las botas de goma	lass BOtass de GOma
rude	mal educado(a)	mal edooKAdo(a)
ruler	la regla	la RRREgla
to run	correr	koRRRER
to run away	escapar	esskaPAR
to run a bath	poner el baño	poNER el BANyo
running shoes	las zapatillas	lass ssapaTEELyass
runway	la pista de aterrizaje	la PEEsta de aterrreeSSAche
Russia	Rusia	ROOsya

S

English	Spanish	Pronunciation
sad	triste	TREEsste
safety belt	el cinturón de seguridad	el sseentooRONN de ssegooreeDAD
sailor	el marinero	el mareeNEro
salad	la ensalada	la enssaLAda
salami	el salami	el saLAmee
salary, wages	el salario	el ssaLARyo
sale	saldos (m. pl)	SSALdoss
sales assistant (m)	el vendedor	el bendeDOR
sales assistant (f)	la vendedora	la bendeDOra
sales representative (m/f)	el/la representante comercial	el/la rrrepressenTANte komerSSYAL
salt	la sal	la ssal
same	igual	eeGWAL
the same age	la misma edad	la MEESma eDAD
sand	la arena	la aRENa
sandals	las sandalias	lass ssanDAlyass
sandcastle	el castillo de arena	el kassTEELyo de aRENa
Saturday	sábado (m)	SSAbado
saucepan	la cacerola	la kasseROla
saucer	el platito	el plaTEEto
sausage	la salchicha	la ssalTSHEEtsha
spicy sausage	el chorizo	el tshoREEsso
saw	la sierra	la SSYErrra
to say	decir	deSSEER
scales	la báscula	la BASSkoola
Scandinavia	Escandinavia	esskandeeNAbya
scarecrow	el espantapájaros	el esspantaPAchaross
scarf	la bufanda	la booFANda
scenery	el decorado	el dekoRAdo
school	el colegio	el koLEchyo
at school	en el colegio	en el koLEchyo
grade school	la escuela primaria	la essKWEla preeMArya
high school	el colegio	el koLEchyo
scissors	las tijeras	lass teeCHErass
to score a goal	meter un gol	meTER oon gol
screw	el tornillo	el torNEElyo

English	Spanish	Pronunciation
screwdriver	el destornillador	el desstorneelyaDOR
sea	el mar	el mar
sea bream	el besugo	el beSSOOgo
seagull	la gaviota	la gabyOta
season	la estación	la esstaSSYONN
season ticket	el billete de abono	el beeLYEte de aBOno
seasoning	el condimento	el kondeeMENto
seat	el asiento	el aSSYENto
seat (cinema, theatre)	la butaca	la booTAka
reserved seat	asiento reservado	aSSYENto rrresserBAdo
seaweed	las algas marinas	lass ALgass maREEnass
second (time)	el segundo	el sseGOONdo
second	segundo(a)	sseGOOndo(a)
the second (date)	el dos	el doss
second class	segunda clase	sseGOOnda KLAsse
second floor	segundo piso	sseGOOndo PEEso
secretary (m)	el secretario	el ssekreTAryo
secretary (f)	la secretaria	la ssekreTArya
See you later	¡Hasta pronto!	ASSta PRONto
seeds	las semillas	lass sseMEELyass
to sell	vender	benDER
to send	mandar	manDAR
I am sending... separately.	Te mando por separado...	te MANdo por ssepaRAdo
to send a postcard	mandar una postal	manDAR oona posTAL
to send a telegram	mandar un telegrama	manDAR oon teleGRAma
sentence	la frase	la FRAsse
September	setiembre	sseTYEMbre
to serve	servir	sserBEER
to set the table	poner la mesa	poNER la MEssa
seven	siete	SSYEte
seventeen	diecisiete	dyesseeSSYEte
seventy	setenta	sseTENta
to sew	coser	koSSER
shade	la sombra	la SSOMbra
to shake	sacudir	sakooDEER
to shake hands	dar la mano	dar la MAno
shallow	poco profundo(a)	POko proFOOndo(a)
shampoo	el champú	el tshamPOO
shape	la forma	la FORma
to shave	afeitarse	afeyTARsse
shaving cream	la espuma de afeitar	la essPOOma de afeyTAR
sheep	la oveja	la oBEcha
sheepdog	el perro pastor	el PErrro passTOR
sheet	la sábana	la SSAbana
shells	las conchitas	la konTSHEEtass
shellfish	los mariscos	loss maREESSkoss
to shine	brillar	breeLYAR
The sun's shining.	Brilla el sol.	BREELya el sol
ship	el barco	el BARko
shirt	la camisa	la kaMEEssa
shoes	los zapatos	loss ssaPAtoss
running shoes	las zapatillas	lass ssapaTEELyas
to go shopping	ir de compras	eer de KOMprass
shopping bag	la bolsa de las compras	la BOLssa de lass KOMprass
short	corto(a)	KORto(a)
to be short	ser bajo	sser BAcho

123

shoulder	el hombro	el OMbro
to shout	gritar	greeTAR
shower	la ducha	la DOOtsha
to take a shower	ducharse	dooTSHARsse
with shower	con ducha	kon DOOtsha
shut	cerrado(a)	sseRRRAdo(a)
shy	tímido(a)	TEEmeedo
side	el lado	el LAdo
side street	la bocacalle	la bokaKAlye
sidewalk	la acera	la aSSEra
to sightsee	visitar los lugares de interés	beesseeTAR loss looGAress de eenteRESS
sign	la señal	la sseNYAL
silly	tonto(a)	TONto(a)
silver	la plata	la PLAta
made of silver	de plata	de PLAta
to sing	cantar	kanTAR
to sing out of tune	cantar desafinado	kanTAR dessafeeNAdo
singer (m/f)	el/la cantante	el/la kanTANte
single room	la habitación individual	la abeetaSSYONN eendeebeeDWAL
sink	el fregadero	el fregaDEro
sister	la hermana	la erMAna
to sit down	sentarse	ssenTARsse
to be sitting down	estar sentado(a)	essTAR ssenTAdo(a)
to sit by the fire	sentarse al fuego	ssenTARsse al FWEgo
six	seis	sseyss
sixteen	dieciséis	dyesseeSEYSS
sixty	sesenta	sseSSENta
size (clothes)	la talla	la TAlya
What size is this?	¿Qué talla es esto?	ke TAlya ess ESSto
to ski	esquiar	esskeeAR
skis	los esquís	loss essKEESS
ski boots	las botas de esquí	lass BOtass de essKEE
ski instructor (m)	el instructor de esquí	el eensstrookTOR de essKEE
ski instructor (f)	la instructora de esquí	la eensstrookTOra de essKEE
ski lift	la telesilla	la teleSSEElya
ski pole	el bastón de esquí	el bassTON de essKEE
ski resort	el centro de esquí	el SSENtro de essKEE
ski slope, ski run	la pista	la PEEssta
skillful, good with your hands	hábil	Abeel
skin	la piel	la pyel
skirt	la falda	la FALda
sky	el cielo	el SSYElo
skyscraper	el rascacielos	el rrraskaSSYEloss
to sleep	dormir	dorMEER
Sleep well.	¡Que duerman bien! (pl)	ke DWERman byen
sleeping bag	la bolsa de dormir	la BOLssa de dorMEER
sleeping car	el coche-cama	el kotsheKAma
slide	el tobogán	el toboGANN
slim	delgado(a)	delGAdo(a)
to slip	resbalar	rrresbaLAR
full slip	la combinación	la combeenaSSYONN
half slip	las enaguas	lass enAgwass
slippers	las zapatillas	lass ssapaTEELyass
slope	la cuesta	la KWEssta

slow	lento(a)	LENto(a)
to slow down	reducir velocidad	rrredooSSEER belosseeDAD
small	chico(a)	TSHEEko(a)
to smell sweet	oler bien	oLER byen
to smile	sonreír	ssonreEER
smoke	el humo	el OOmo
smokestack	la chimenea	la tsheemeNEya
snake	la serpiente	la sserPYENte
to sneeze	estornudar	esstornooDAR
to snore	roncar	rrronKAR
snow	la nieve	la NYEbe
It's snowing.	Nieva.	NYEba
snowman	el muñeco de nieve	el mooNYEko de NYEbe
to be soaked to the skin	estar calado(a)	essTAR kaLAdo(a)
soap	el jabón	el chaBONN
soccer ball	el balón	el baLONN
to play soccer	jugar al fútbol	chooGAR al FOODbol
society	la sociedad	la ssossyeDAD
socks	los calcetines	loss kalsseTEEness
sofa	el sofá	el ssoFA
soft (smooth)	suave	SSWAbe
soft (not hard)	blando(a)	BLANdo(a)
soil	la tierra	la TYErrra
soldier	el soldado	el ssolDAdo
soloist	el/la solista	el/la soLEEsta
someone	alguien	ALgyen
son	el hijo	el EEcho
to sort, to arrange	ordenar	ordeNAR
soup	la sopa	la SSOpa
south	el sur	el ssoor
South Pole	el polo sur	el POlo ssoor
to sow	sembrar	ssemBRAR
space	el espacio	el essPAssyo
spaceship	la nave espacial	la NAbe esspaSSYAL
spade	la pala	la PAla
Spain	España	la essPANya
Spanish (language, subject)	el español	el esspanYOL
sparrow	el gorrión	el goRRRYONN
spelling	la ortografía	la ortograFEEya
to spend money	gastar dinero	gasTAR deeNEro
spider	la araña	la aRANya
spinach	las espinacas	lass esspeeNAkass
to splash	salpicar	salpeeKAR
spoon	la cuchara	la kooTSHAra
sports	el deporte	el dePORte
sports equipment	los artículos de deportes	loss arTEEkooloss de dePORtess
spotlight	el foco	el FOko
spotted	con lunares	kon looNAress
to sprain your wrist	dislocarse la muñeca	deesloKARsse la mooNYEka
spring	la primavera	la preemaBEra
square (shape)	el cuadrado	el kwaDRAdo
square (in town)	la plaza	la PLAssa
to play squash	jugar al squash	chooGAR al skwash
squirrel	la ardilla	la arDEElya
stable	la cuadra	la KWAdra
stage (theatre)	el escenario	el esseNAryo
staircase, stairs	la escalera	la esskaLEra
stamp	el sello	el SSELyo
to stand in line	hacer cola	aSSER KOla

English	Spanish	Pronunciation
to stand up	pararse	paRARsse
to be standing	estar parado(a)	eSSTAR paRAdo(a)
star	la estrella	la essTRElya
to start the car	arrancar	arrranKAR
station	la estación	la esstaSSYONN
statue	la estatua	la essTAtooa
to stay in a hotel	quedarse en un hotel	keDARsse en oon oTEL
steak	el filete	el feeLEte
to steal	robar	rrroBAR
steep	empinado(a)	empeeNAdo(a)
steering wheel	el volante	el boLANte
stewardess	la azafata	la assaFAta
to stick	pegar	peGAR
to sting	picar	peeKAr
stomach	el estómago	el essTOmago
to have a stomach ache	tener dolor de estómago	teNER doLOR de essTOmago
store	la tienda	la TYENda
storekeeper (m)	el tendero	el tenDEro
storekeeper (f)	la tendera	la tenDEra
store window	el escaparate	el esskapaRAte
storm	la tormenta	la torMENta
story	el cuento	el KWENto
straight (hair)	lacio(a)	LEEso(a)
to have straight hair	tener el pelo lacio	teNER el PElo LAssyo
to go straight	seguir todo derecho	sseGEER TOdo deREtsho
strawberry	la fresa	la FREssa
stream	el arroyo	el aRRROyo
street	la calle	la KAlye
side street	la bocacalle	la bokaKAlye
street light	el poste de la luz	el POSSte de la looss
to stretch	estirarse	essteeRARsse
stretcher	la camilla	la kaMEElya
striped	a rayas	a RRRAyass
stroller	el cochecito	el kotsheSSEEto
strong	fuerte	FWERte
student (m/f)	el/la estudiante	el/la esstooDYANte
to study	estudiar	esstooDYAR
stylist (establishment)	la peluquería	la pelookeREEya
stylist (m)	el peluquero	el pelooKEro
stylist (f)	la peluquera	la pelooKEra
subject (of study)	la materia	la maTErya
to subtract	restar	rrresSTAR
suburbs	las afueras	lass aFWErass
subway (street crossing)	el paso subterráneo	el PAsso soobteRRRAnyo
subway (train)	el metro	el MEtro
subway station	la estación de metro	la esstaSSYONN de MEtro
sugar	el azúcar	el aSSOOkar
suitcase	la maleta	la maLEta
summer	el verano	el beRAno
summit	la cima	la SSEEma
sun	el sol	el ssol
The sun's shining.	Brilla el sol.	BREElya el ssol
to sunbathe	tomar sol	toMAR ssol
Sunday	domingo (m)	doMEENGgo
sunglasses	las gafas de sol	lass GAfass de ssol
sunrise	la salida del sol	la ssaLEEda del ssol
sunset	la puesta del sol	la PWESSta del ssol
suntan lotion	la crema bronceadora	la KREma bronsseaDOra

English	Spanish	Pronunciation
supermarket	el supermercado	el soopermerKAdo
to go to the supermarket	ir al supermercado	eer al soopermerKAdo
surgeon	el cirujano	el sseerooCHAno
surname	el apellido	el apelLYEEdo
to sweat	sudar	sooDAR
sweet (tasting)	dulce	DOOLsse
sweet, charming	encantador(a)	enkantaDOR(a)
to swim	nadar	naDAR
swimming pool	la piscina	la peeSSEEna
swing	el columpio	el koLOOMpyo
Switzerland	Suiza	SSWEEssa

T

table	la mesa	la MEssa
bedside table	la mesilla de noche	la meSSEElya de NOtshe
to lay the table	poner la mesa	poNER la MEssa
tablecloth	el mantel	el manTEL
tail	el rabo	el RRRAbo
to take	tomar	toMAR
to take a bath	bañarse	banYARsse
to take the bus	tomar el camión	toMAR el kaMYONN
to take an exam	dar un examen	dar oon ekSAmen
to take off	despegar	desspeGAR
to take out	sacar	ssaKAR
to take money out of the bank	sacar dinero del banco	ssaKAR deeNEro del BANko
to take a photograph	tomar una foto	toMAR OOna FOto
to take someone's pulse	tomar el pulso	toMAR el POOLsso
to take a shower	ducharse	dooTSHARsse
to take someone's temperature	tomar la temperatura	toMAR la temperaTOOra
to take the train	tomar el tren	toMAR el tren
to take (a dog) for a walk	llevar a pasear	lyeBAR a passeAR
to be tall	ser alto	sser ALto(a)
tame	manso(a)	MANsso(a)
tanned	bronceado(a)	bronsseAdo(a)
tart	la tarta	la TARta
taste, flavour	el sabor	el ssaBOR
to taste, try	probar	proBAR
It tastes good.	Está muy rico.	essTA mooy RRREEko
taxes	los impuestos	loss eemPWESStoss
taxi	el taxi	el TAKssee
taxi driver	el taxista	el takSSEESSta
taxi rank	la parada de taxis	la paRAda de TAKsseess
to hail a taxi	parar un taxi	paRAR oon TAKssee
tea	el té	el te
tea towel	el trapo de la cocina	el TRApo de la koSSEEna
to teach	enseñar	enssenYAR
teacher (m)	el profesor	el profeSSOR
teacher (f)	la profesora	la profeSSOra
team	el equipo	el eKEEpo
teapot	la tetera	la teTEra
to tear	rasgar	rrrasGAR
telegram	el telegrama	el teleGRAma
telephone	el teléfono	el teLEfono

English	Spanish	Pronunciation
telephone call	la llamada	la lyaMAda
to make a telephone call	hacer una llamada	aSSER OOna lyaMAda
telephone directory	la guía telefónica	la GEEya teleFOneeka
telephone number	el número de teléfono	el NOOmero de teLEfono
telescope	el telescopio	el telessKOpyo
television	la televisión	la telebeeSSYONN
to have a temperature	tener fiebre	teNER FYEbre
to take someone's temperature	tomar la temperatura	toMAR la temperaTOOra
ten	diez	dyess
tenant (m)	el inquilino	el eenkeeLEEno
tenant (f)	la inquilino	la eenkeeLEEna
tennis court	la cancha de tenis	la KANtsha de TEneess
tennis player (m/f)	el/la tenista	el/la teNEESSta
to play tennis	jugar al tenis	chooGAR al TEneess
tent	la tienda de campaña	la TYENda de kamPANya
to thank	dar las gracias	dar lass GRAssyass
Thank you for your letter of...	Gracias por su carta del...	GRAssyass por ssoo KARta del...
Thank you very much.	¡Muchas gracias!	MOOtshass GRAssyass
That will be... (cost)	Son...	ssonn
theater	el teatro	el teAtro
then	entonces	enTONssess
thermometer	el termómetro	el terMOmetro
thin	flaco(a)	FLAko(a)
a third	una tercera parte	OOna terSSEra PARte
the third (date)	el tres	el tress
to be thirsty	tener sed	teNER ssed
thirteen	trece	TREsse
thirty	treinta	TREYeenta
this afternoon, evening	esta tarde	ESSta TARde
this morning	esta mañana	ESSta manYAna
a thousand	mil	meel
thread	el hilo	el EElo
three	tres	tress
three quarters	tres cuartos	tress KWARtoss
the Three Wise Men	los Reyes Magos	loss RRREyess MAgoss
through	por	por
to throw	echar, tirar	eTSHAR, teeRAR
thrush	el zorzal	el ssorSSAL
thumb	el pulgar	el poolGAR
thunder	los truenos	loss trooWEnoss
Thursday	jueves (m)	chooWEbess
ticket	el boleto	el boLEto
local ticket (in city)	el boleto urbano	el boLEto oorBAno
round trip ticket	el boleto de ida y vuelta	el boLEto de EEda ee BWELta
season ticket	el boleto de abono	el boLEto de aBOno
ticket collector	el revisor	el rebeeSSOR
ticket machine	la máquina de boletos	la MAkeena de boLEtoss
ticket office	la taquilla	la taKEElya
to tidy up	ordenar	ordeNAR
tie	la corbata	la korBAta
tiger	el tigre	el TEEgre
tight	apretado(a)	apreTAdo
time	el tiempo	el TYEMpo
What time is it?	¿Qué hora es?	ke Ora ess
times (maths)	por	por
timetable	el horario	el oRAreeo
tiny	diminuto(a)	deemeeNOOto(a)
tip	la propina	la proPEEna
Is the tip included?	¿Está incluido el servicio?	essTA eenklooEEdo el sserBEEssyo
The tip is not included.	El servicio no está incluido.	el sserBEEssyo no essTA eenklooEEdo
tire	el neumático	el neooMAteeko
to have a flat tire	tener una rueda desinflada	teNER OOna RWEda desseenFLAda
to be tired	estar cansado(a)	essTAR kanSSAdo
to, toward	hacia	Assya
toboggan	el trineo	el treeNEo
today	hoy	oy
toe	el dedo del pie	el DEdo del pyE
together	juntos(as)	CHOONtoss(ass)
tomato	el tomate	el toMAte
tomorrow	mañana	manYAna
tomorrow afternoon	mañana por la tarde	manYAna por la TARde
tomorrow morning	mañana por la mañana	manYAna por la manYAna
tongue	la lengua	la LENGgwa
tooth	el diente	el DYENte
to have toothache	tener dolor de muelas	teNER doLOR de MWElass
toothbrush	el cepillo de dientes	el ssePEELyo de DYENtess
toothpaste	la pasta de dientes	la PASSta de DYENtess
tortoise	la tortuga	la torTOOga
to touch	tocar	toKAR
tour bus	el autobús	el aootoBOOS
tourist (m/f)	el/la turista	el/la tooREESSta
towel	la toalla	la toAlya
town	la ciudad	la sseeooDAD
town hall	el municipio	el mooneeSSEEpyo
toy	el juguete	el chooGEte
track	la vía	la BEEya
tracksuit	el equipo de deporte	el eKEEpo de dePORte
tractor	el tractor	el trakTOR
traffic	el tráfico	el TRAfeeko
traffic jam	el embotellamiento	el embotellaMYENto
traffic lights	el semáforo	el sseMAforo
train	el tren	el tren
intercity train	el tren interurbano	el tren eenteroorBAno
The train from...	El tren desde...	el tren DESde
The train to...	El tren para...	el tren PAra
trash bin	el basurero	el basooREro
to travel by boat, to sail	ir en barco	eer en BARko
traveler (m)	el viajero	el beeaCHEro
traveler (f)	la viajera	la beeaCHEra
tray	la bandeja	la banDEcha
tree	el árbol	el ARbol
triangle	el triángulo	el treeANgoolo
trowel	la paleta	la paLEta
truck	el camión	el kaMYONN
truck driver	el camionero	el kamyoNEro

true	verdadero(a)	berdaDEro(a)
trumpet	la trompeta	la tromPEta
to play the trumpet	tocar la trompeta	toKAR la tromPEta
trunk (of car)	el portaequipajes	el portaekeePAchess
trunk (elephant)	la trompa	la TROMpa
T-shirt	la camiseta	la kameeSSEta
Tuesday	martes (m)	MARtess
Tuesday, the second of June	martes, dos de junio	MARtess, doss de CHOOnyo
tulip	el tulipán	el tooleePAN
tune	la melodía	la meloDEEya
to turn	doblar	doBLAR
to turn left	doblar a la izquierda	doBLAR a la eessKYErda
to turn off the light	apagar	apaGAR
to turn on the light	encender la luz	enssenDER la looss
to turn right	doblar a la derecha	doBLAR a la deREtsha
turn signal	el indicador	el eendeekaDOR
tusk	el colmillo	el kolMEElyo
twelve	doce	DOsse
twenty	veinte	BEYeente
twin brothers (or twin brother and sister)	los gemelos	loss cheMEloss
twin sisters	las gemelas	lass cheMElass
two	dos	doss

U

umbrella	el paraguas	el paRAgwass
uncle	el tío	el TEEyo
under	debajo de	deBAcho de
underpants	los calzoncillos	loss kalssonSSEELyoss
to get undressed	quitarse la ropa	keeTARsse la RRROpa
unemployment	el desempleo	el desemPLEo
United States	los Estados Unidos	loss essTAdoss ooNEEdoss
universe	el universo	el ooneeBERsso
university	la universidad	la ooneebersseeDAD
to unload	descargar	desskarGAR
up	arriba	aRRREEba
to get up	levantarse	lebanTARsse
upstairs	arriba	aRRREEba
Urgent message stop telephone home	Mensaje urgente punto llamar a casa	menSSAche oorCHENte POONto lyaMAR a CAssa
useful	útil	OOteel
usherette	la acomodadora	la akomodaDOra

V

vacation	las vacaciones	lass bakaSSYOness
to go on vacation	ir de vacaciones	eer de bacaSSYOness
to vacuum	pasar la aspiradora	paSSAR la asspeeraDOra
valley	el valle	el BAlye
van	la camioneta	la kamyoNEta
veal	la ternera	la terNEra
vegetable garden	la huerta	la WERta

vegetables	las verduras	lass berDOORass
Very well, thank you.	Muy bien, gracias	mooy byen GRAssyass
vest	la camiseta	la kameeSSEta
video	el vídeo	el BEEdeo
video camera	la máquina de vídeo	la MAkeena de BEEdeo
view	la vista	la BEEssta
village	el pueblo	el PWEBlo
vine	la vid	la beed
vinegar	el vinagre	el beeNAgre
vineyard	la viña	la BEENya
violin	el violín	el beeoLEEN
to play the violin	tocar el violín	toKAr el beeoLEEN
volume	el volumen	el boLOOmen
to vote	votar	boTAR

W

to wag its tail	mover el rabo	moBER el RRRAbo
to wait for	esperar	esspeRAR
waiter	el mesero	el meSSEro
waiting-room	la sala de espera	la SSAla DE essPEra
to wake up	despertarse	dessperTARsse
walk	el paseo	el paSSEo
to walk, go on foot	ir a pie	eer a pyE
to walk barefoot	andar descalzo	anDAR dessKALsso(a)
to go for a walk	dar un paseo	dar oon paSSEyo
to take (a dog) for a walk	llevar a pasear	lyeBAR a passeAR
wall	la pared	la paRED
wall-to-wall carpet	la alfombra de pared a pared	la alFOMbra de paRED a paRED
to wash the dishes	lavar los platos	laBAR loss PLAtoss
to wash your hair	lavarse el pelo	laBArsse el PElo
to wash oneself	lavarse	laBARsse
washcloth	la toallita	la toalYEEta
washing machine	la lavadora	la labaDOra
washroom	el baño	el BANyo
wasp	la avispa	la aBEESSpa
watch	el reloj de pulsera	el rrreLOCH de poolSSEra
to watch television	ver la televisión	ber la telebeeSSYONN
water	el agua (f)	el Agwa
cold water	el agua fría	el Agwa FREEya
hot water	el agua (f) caliente	el Agwa caLYENte
mineral water	el agua (f) mineral	el Agwa meeneRAL
watering can	la regadera	la rrregaDEra
to waterski	hacer esquí acuático	aSSER essKEE aKWAteeko
wave	la ola	la Ola
way, path	el camino	el kaMEEno
to ask the way	preguntar el camino	pregoonTAR el kaMEEno
Which way is…?	¿Por dónde está?	por DONde essTA DEbeel
weak	débil	DEbeel
to wear	llevar	lyeBAR
to wear glasses	llevar gafas	lyeBAR GAfass
weather	el tiempo	el TYEMpo
weather forecast	el pronóstico del tiempo	el proNOSSteeko del TYEMpo

What's the weather like?	¿Qué tiempo hace?	ke TYEMpo Asse
wedding	la boda	la BOda
wedding ring	la alianza	la aleeANssa
Wednesday	miércoles (m)	MYERkoless
weeds	la maleza	la maLEssa
to weed	arrancar la maleza	arrranKAR la maLEssa
week	la semana	la sseMAna
weekend	el fin de semana	el feen de sseMAna
weeping willow	el sauce llorón	el SSAOOsse lyoRONN
to weigh	pesar	peSSAR
to weigh yourself	pesarse	peSSARsse
weight	el peso	el PEsso
well	bien	byen
to have eaten well	haber comido bien	aBER koMEEdo byen
Very well, thank you.	Muy bien, gracias.	mooy byen GRAssyass
west	el oeste	el oESSte
What's the weather like?	¿Qué tiempo hace?	ke TYEMpo Asse
What size is this?	¿Qué talla es esto?	ke TAlya ess ESSto
What time is it?	¿Qué hora es?	ke Ora ess
What would you like?	¿Qué van a tomar?	ke ban a toMAR
What's your name?	¿Cómo te llamas?	KOmo te LYAmass
wheat	el trigo	el TREEgo
wheel	la rueda	la RWEda
wheelbarrow	la carretilla	la karrreTEELya
Which way is...?	¿Por dónde está?	por DONde essTA
to whisper	cuchichear	kootsheetsheAR
white	blanco(a)	BLANko
Who's speaking?	¿Quién habla?	kyen Abla
width	el ancho	el ANtsho
wife	la esposa	la essPOssa
wild	salvaje	ssalBAche
wild flowers	las flores silvestres	lass FLOress sseelBESStress
to win	ganar	gaNAR
wind	el viento	el BYENto
It's windy.	Hace viento.	Asse BYENto
window	la ventana	la benTAna
to go window-shopping	ir de escaparates	eer de esscapaRAtess
windshield	el parabrisas	el paraBREESSass
to windsurf	hacer windsurf	aSSER WEENsoorf
wine	el vino	el BEEno
wing	el ala (f)	el Ala
winter	el invierno	el eenBYerno
with	con	kon
with balcony	con balcón	kon balKONN

with shower	con ducha	kon DOOtsha
without	sin	sseen
woman	la mujer	la mooCHER
wood (trees)	el bosque	el BOSSke
wood (material)	la madera	la maDEra
wooden, made of wood	de madera	de maDEra
woodwork	la carpintería	la karpeenteREEya
wool (yarn)	la lana	la LAna
wool, made of wool	de lana	de LAna
word	la palabra	la paLAbra
to work	trabajar	trabaCHAR
to go to work	ir a trabajar	eer a trabaCHAR
world	el mundo	el MOONdo
wrapping paper	el papel de envolver	el paPEL de enbolBER
wrist	la muñeca	la mooNYEka
to write	escribir	esskreeBEER
to write a check	hacer un cheque	aSSER oon TSHEke
to write a letter	escribir una carta	esskreeBEER OOna KARta
writing paper	el papel de escribir	el paPEL de esskreeBEER

Y

to yawn	bostezar	bossteSSAR
year	el año	el ANyo
yellow	amarillo(a)	amaREELyo(a)
yes	sí	ssee
yesterday	ayer	aYER
yesterday morning	ayer por la mañana	aYER por la manYAna
yogurt	el yogur	el yoGOOR
young, little	chico(a)	TSHEEko(a)
younger than	menor	meNOR
Yours faithfully,	Le saluda atentamente,	le ssaLOOda atentaMENte

Z

zebra	la cebra	la SSEbra
zero	cero	SSEro
zip code	el código postal	el KOdeego possTAL
zipper	la cremallera	la kremaLYEra
zoo	el zoológico	el ssooLOcheeko
zoo keeper	el guardián	el gwarDYAN

First published in 1988 by Usborne Publishing Ltd Usborne House, 83-85 Saffron Hill, London EC1N 8RT England. www.usborne.com
Copyright © 2002, 1998, 1988 Usborne Publishing Ltd.

Printed in Dubai by Oriental Press

This American edition 2003.